THE
FAMILY
TRAVEL
HANDBOOK

Everything you need to know to take
unforgettable trips with your children

© WESTEND61 / GETTY IMAGES

CONTENTS

© KLAUS VEDFELT / GETTY IMAGES

The family travel challenge!

Does taking a trip with your kids in tow feel like running a constant gauntlet, or too daunting to even contemplate? While there's no one-size-fits-all answer, a willingness to explore and go on adventures with your children opens up a rich world of possibilities.

Travel broadens our minds, develops cultural empathy and gives us a better understanding of the world. We travel with our children because we believe these experiences not only improve their social skills but are key to helping them become engaged global citizens.

We also travel with our kids because it's really fun! It's an amazing experience to see the world together as a family. We talk and share experiences which create strong bonds and shared memories.

Travelling with children makes you slow down and appreciate different things – the questions they ask that you've never thought of, the need for an unscheduled pit stop which leads to the discovery of a new place, watching kids communicate with instant friends in the local park despite no shared language. We watch our children grow as they respond to new adventures and the challenges of travelling, and we grow ourselves as our own travel experience is enriched by their reactions.

However, no one is going to tell you that travelling with kids is glamorous, easy or relaxing. Whether you are thinking about taking your baby on a plane for the first time or you're planning a final epic road

to family travel. There is no one 'right' way to start exploring the world with your kids; each family has to figure out what works best for them as they travel. Doing so takes some grit and determination, and also acceptance that sometimes you will make the wrong decision and learn from it. Those 'travel fails' are almost as important for family folklore as trips where everything goes swimmingly and you get to share the travel buzz.

However, that's not to say that you can't learn from others' experiences. And that's where this book comes in. Lonely Planet's founders Tony and Maureen Wheeler travelled with their own kids as they set up the company in the 1970s, and every day our writers and staffers share tips and recommendations focused on travel with kids. Collectively we've covered thousands of miles with our

children, from making the most of a local day trip to biking across continents, from a short trip to another city to relaxing on a farm stay in the middle of the countryside, and from learning to ski to enjoying the spectacle of a Disney cruise. You name it, we've probably done it. Now we're sharing the knowledge we've gained from our experiences with you in this book.

Our aim is to bring together all of our expertise in one useful handbook that you can refer to as much for ideas about exploring the great outdoors close to home as for advice on packing up everything and taking the kids on a round-the-world trip. Your family may be experienced jet-setters, or you may be unsure where to start when taking your kids on the road, but amazing opportunities for travelling together exist at every turn.

trip with reluctant teenagers before they fly the nest, each and every time you travel as a family you take on a challenge. The challenge of coordinating different needs, different desires and different personalities into one perfect trip where everyone has an amazing time. Because that's the ultimate aim, isn't it? To finish a trip feeling happy, refreshed and full of new stories. After all, there are many reasons we travel but it's the buzz you get from a positive experience exploring somewhere new that drives many of us to share our love of travel with our children.

As with parenting itself, we all have different approaches

© MUHA / GETTY IMAGES

The changing landscape of family travel

© JURGAR / GETTY IMAGES

Travel has never been so child-friendly. Long gone are the days when in-flight entertainment was limited to one communal screen, museums hid all their fascinating wares behind glass, and dining out at fancy restaurants was an adults-only affair. Now you can fly wherever you want to (and often for reasonable fares), there's a huge range of accommodation options for travelling families, and many more sights and attractions are geared towards entertaining small people. And that's without even mentioning the benefits of technology. Digital maps, translation apps and games for the kids all make life on the road much less stressful than was previously the case.

IT'S ALL ABOUT THE LITTLE ONES

No longer an afterthought, now children are specifically catered to as a group with very distinct needs by attractions of all kinds. Museums and art galleries in particular have upped their game with kid-friendly tours, interactive exhibits and a much more tolerant approach to the occasional squawk from a toddler. Many restaurants offer children's menus (sometimes plus colouring pens and paper) as standard, and big airlines such as Emirates offer kids activity packs. And of course, in-flight entertainment now gives each member of the family the ability to choose what they want to watch, listen to or play.

WE ALL SLEEP EASIER, FAMILY STYLE

The improvement in accommodation options for families in the last decade or so has been marked. Hotels are generally far better prepared for families, offering adjoining rooms, cots and even babysitting services. Plus there's a whole range of luxury properties created specifically for the family market with kids clubs, child-friendly menus, play areas and on-site entertainment. Thanks to popular home swap and rental sites it's now super easy for families to locate great apartments, often with toys, bunk beds and more. Taking it up a level, family-friendly cruises, safaris and sleeper trains all offer unique and interesting ways for families to spend their nights.

OUR CHILDREN ARE DIGITAL NATIVES

Technology has transformed how children engage with a trip. Sure, the tech-free pursuits still apply – kids from any era adore reading, writing, drawing and playing games. But now they supplement these with a wealth of digital aids: translation apps to converse easily with locals; search engines to locate fun things to do; and Skype or social media to share stories with family and friends back home. Tablets are now key weapons in the parental arsenal against 'I'm bored': they get families through delays and meltdowns, and provide respite for siblings who need a bit of space from each other. Just don't forget to pack the charger (and a converter if needed!).

© YULIA PORKOVA / GETTY IMAGES

© JONATHAN STOKES / LONELY PLANET

What type of trip is

Different experiences suit different families. You can explore a new city, camp in the midst of nature, ski down a mountain slope, or immerse yourself in another language and culture. Different experiences suit different families and stages of life, and there are plenty of options to explore together.

TAKE A STAYCATION

FIND A BASE AND EXPLORE

BE ACTIVE

Travel is about exploring the world, whether it's on your doorstep or 1000 miles away. Staying at home but pretending to be on holiday by taking a staycation can really fire everyone's imagination. Take time off work, forget the chores, put down the devices and take each day as it comes like you would if you were out of town. This is your chance to visit the museum you've been meaning to take the kids to for ages, hike that trail you always talk about or try a new spot that's supposed to have great ice cream.

One of the gentlest introductions to travelling with kids is to rent a home, from an apartment to a cottage or even a villa. With a kitchen available, you can make meals at home. Or, if your bank balance allows it, the holy grail might just be a private place with someone else to do the cooking. Having your own space allows the whole family to breathe out and not worry about being on best behaviour the whole time. For younger children you can often find places with toys, and most will offer wi-fi (which can always be 'broken' if required.)

As children get older and are physically able to join in with more activities, a trip which centres around being active can be a fantastic way to bond as a family. The sense of achievement for the whole family of getting everyone hiking to the top of a mountain, cycling round that lake or skiing down a slope together is the stuff that cements your family unit. There's usually a fair bit of planning (and a fair bit of parental patience) involved to make sure that you can all get involved safely and happily but it pays off.

best for your family?

MAKE A (CITY) BREAK FOR IT

GET BEHIND THE WHEEL

GIVE BACK

Many cities have an incredible array of child-friendly attractions and plenty of accessible places to eat. Others are hectic, noisy and polluted, factors which might not feature highly on your wish list for a trip with your kids. Chosen wisely, a city break with kids is incredibly rewarding in terms of watching them immerse themselves in a new city's culture and can work especially well for older kids, who get to help navigate the transit system.

Travelling for hours in a car with small children can bring its own challenges, but packing the family up and setting off with everything you need, a good playlist and a bucket load of road trip snacks is a family adventure in itself. You may need to factor in more regular stops, prepare an arsenal of age-appropriate games and accept the back of your car looking like a bomb has hit it, but the kids will share your feelings of freedom and can even suggest stops en route.

Travelling is one of the best ways to expose children to the wider world and encourage them to be understanding, tolerant and flexible when dealing with others. Getting involved in a volunteering programme either at home or abroad consolidates this understanding and teaches families to work together, have empathy and appreciate what they have. Make sure you do your research to make sure you're working with a reputable organisation.

What are you worried about?

Deciding to venture far beyond the structured environment of home isn't easy. Even the most hardened of family travellers suffer from anxiety when planning and undertaking a trip. Here we tackle the four most common parent concerns.

CAN WE KEEP THEM HEALTHY AND SAFE IF WE TAKE THEM AWAY?

New parents spend a not inconsiderable amount of time thinking about protecting their young charges from harm. Each day is a risk mitigation exercise, and working out how to accept it when things go wrong is all part of the journey. When we travel we deal with more elements that are out of our control and we're often facing the unknown. Add that to the list of worries we already face as parents and it's a wonder we even step out of the front door with our kids, let alone take them off to new lands. While the leap is definitely worth taking, when it comes to health and safety there are some basic things you can do to help prepare yourself. Remind yourself that children can get sick or hurt wherever they are, even in the backyard. And as much as possible, be prepared for any eventuality.

Depending on where you are travelling to, you may need to book vaccinations or organise anti-malarial medication; it's best not to leave this until the last minute. Wherever you are going, take a first aid course so you can remember what you should do if you are first on the scene and carry a basic first aid kit in your day pack. Make a note of emergency numbers in the country you are visiting and talk to your kids about basic hygiene, road crossing (especially in places where they drive on a different side of the road to at home) and listening to instructions. You may have said it all before over and over, but reminding them of the simple ways they can protect themselves never hurts, even if they are teenagers and have been looking after themselves independently for years. Depending on your child's needs, countries with less established medical infrastructures may not be the right choice for your family just yet, but there are plenty of regions where you can be safe in the knowledge you would get good care if your family needed it.

To help your peace of mind, always make sure you have travel insurance. It is not worth the risk to travel without it, however much you feel like it's a wasted expenditure when you get home again not having used it. Better safe than sorry is a wise adage for travelling families. Imagine you're in an emergency situation and have to fly someone home. You will be so grateful you didn't scrimp on the insurance.

WHAT HAPPENS IF WE'RE INVOLVED IN AN EMERGENCY?

Natural disasters, terrorist attacks and unexpected crises abroad are random events and statistically your family are unlikely to be involved in one. As experts often cite, you are more likely to be involved in a car accident close to home, and most of us get in and out of cars very regularly. However, you should absolutely be aware of any current concerns or issues within the destination you are travelling to and follow official advice on areas to avoid (or whether to travel there in the first place). It's important to know your own risk tolerance levels and do your research. If somewhere on your wish list is considered relatively safe by official channels but when you read more details you aren't so sure about taking your kids, maybe it should stay on that wish list for now. There are plenty of other places to explore and it's not worth taking a trip if you are going to be constantly worried about everyone's safety. And if you do your research, weigh up the risks and decide to go ahead, then make sure you relax and enjoy it knowing you've taken everything into account.

The latest travel information can be found at the official government advisory resources below. It's worth reading state advisories and paying attention to aspects of them like no-go areas which can impact whether your travel insurance is valid. Do balance their views with those of family, friends and travellers who may have been to where you're going. Your own comfort level is key in choosing a destination.

© CATHERINE SUTHERLAND / LONELY PLANET

©JUSTIN FOULKES / LONELY PLANET

© IMGORTHAND / GETTY IMAGES

★ **Australian Department of Foreign Affairs and Trade,**
www.smartraveller. gov.au

★ **Global Affairs Canada,**
www.travel.gc.ca

★ **New Zealand Ministry of Foreign Affairs and Trade,**
www.safetravel. govt.nz

★ **UK Foreign & Commonwealth Office,**
www.fco.gov.uk/ travel

★ **US Department of State's Bureau of Consular Affairs,**
www.travel.state. gov

FAMILY TRAVEL HANDBOOK

CAN WE JUSTIFY THE EXPENSE?

While there's ample advice in this book for how to keep the costs of family travel under control, travelling as a family will always involve certain expenditures. You all need to eat food, lay your heads down somewhere safe and relatively comfortable, and depending on your destination you will often have to pay admission costs, which can add up if you have a large family. Family travel has also become noticeably more expensive in recent years. The price hikes for trips during school breaks are well documented but there's also the steady upward trajectory of the costs of food, accommodation and entry to attractions. Travelling off season or to affordable destinations (or utilising mileage points and rewards for booking travel, often the costliest portion) will help.

Only you can work out if the family finances can handle the cost of a trip, but it's important to remember that if you think you can stretch to cover the cost you will rarely regret spending the money. You're investing in both the immediate family bond and the longer-term impact on your collective memory bank. That's definitely worth the money.

IS IT REALLY WORTH ALL THE WORK AND WORRY TO TRAVEL WITH MY KIDS?

Getting ready for a trip with kids in tow is hard work and, when kids are little, you wonder if they will even remember any of it when they are older. But once you are there, together as a family experiencing something new, it can be magic. In little kids, the subconscious memories of adapting to new circumstances and having relaxed and happy parents giving them their full attention will remain with them and help form their personality. As children get older, you are giving them a whole set of extracurricular skills, from reading maps and packing to how to be flexible, tolerant and (dare we say it?) patient. You are also enhancing some of their academic lessons in foreign languages (the importance of), maths (currency, budgeting) and the humanities (what happened in the past, why is the country like it is now, what geographical features can we see?).

So if you want to spend quality time with your children and help them learn, grow and gain a better understanding of the world and humanity and also feed your own travel bug, then give it a try!

You can do it!

Are you reading this book in the dead of night as you feed a new baby, wondering if you will ever travel again? Or are you dipping in as a seasoned family traveller looking for inspiration and new ideas? Or did you have a bad experience last time you took your kids away and you're slowly building your confidence to try again?

Whatever your family's travel backstory, rest easy that you don't have to embark on your family adventures without guidance. In this handbook we tackle the essentials for planning a trip, including advice on dealing with special needs and what to pack. Then we cover the nuts and bolts of physically travelling with your kids, including plenty of ideas for keeping them entertained and sane during long journeys.

Next get advice to help the trip run more smoothly with ideas on eating, accommodation, sight-seeing and exploring the great outdoors. Find prompts for local day trips, staycations and weekends away and then ideas for when you are ready to be more adventurous. We've also got practical suggestions for making the most of the educational opportunities that travel provides, as well as some lovely ideas for how to preserve

and cherish the memories of your trip when you are all back home and into the routines of work and school. Lastly, at the end of the book we have asked ten family travellers to tell us about their experiences of visiting specific destinations, and we've included plenty of themed lists of destinations too.

We know family travel can be challenging; it is also life-

enriching. No matter who you are or what your family looks like, we've got you covered. Whether you're dipping your toe into family travel for the first time or want to refresh yourself on some of the planning principles, come along for the ride. The challenges are more than surmountable, and the rewards are ample. So come along for the ride with our Family Travel Handbook.

© TINA GARCIA / LONELY PLANET

Deciding where to go

A key part of your planning for a family trip is choosing the right destination. Whether you like to book spontaneously or have your next three trips planned far in advance, make sure you've got a good idea about where you want to go and how it will work for your family before you part with any of your hard-earned cash. If your children are in school you will be limited by academic holidays; it makes sense to take longer trips in the longer holidays, but be aware of different climates (for example, if you want to use the US or UK summer holidays to take that trip to Patagonia, it might be cooler than you expect, with some seasonal closures).

If you're home schooling, make the most of not being tied to the school calendar.

Whether you want to go long haul or not, or even fly at all, will be influenced by how you feel about travelling on planes with your children – as well as your budget. Choosing the right destination (and the best way to get there) will pay dividends when it comes to taking the trip. If you are travelling with another family or in a multigenerational group, consider what everyone involved wants and needs. Home rentals you can easily reach often work well for groups, but you'll need to check what things there are to do in the area and agree on

how you plan to manage meals in advance.

If you like culture but the kids want to be active, can you find somewhere that offers you both? If you are travelling with very small people are you more comfortable in a villa with space and the ability to make meals yourself? Or are your kids old enough to trust in a hotel room on their own and do you crave not having to think about every single meal? Communication is key here. Learn from previous trips and talk to each other about what you want to do and what is important. That includes hearing from the kids about their preferences, too!

Travelling independently vs package tours

While travelling independently is definitely a rewarding experience, it's worth considering whether an organised tour is right for your family. Particularly for those families travelling for the first time, visiting a more challenging destination or trying a specific activity or adventure, letting someone else do the logistical legwork can be worth the extra cost. However, the peace of mind you are after does come at a price. Discounts are rarely available for children and the smaller the group, the more customised the package. Similarly, the more adventurous the activities, the higher the overall price.

Most of the major tour operators have excellent family packages which balance cultural visits with fun activities, and unusual means of transport (think camels, tuk-tuks, rafts) with more conventional ones. They may focus on the environment, nature and local culture, or on adventure activities.

As they cater to the needs and interests of all in the group, a package trip can work especially well for multigenerational trips.

When choosing an operator always check their safety record and pick one who focuses on family travel, rather than one which will simply accommodate children. It's also important to choose a responsible operator: check their website for a responsible travel or sustainable tourism policy. If there's nothing set down in writing, chances are they are not taking their obligations to the local community and environment seriously.

Likewise, for some destinations going to a resort can be a good value. Cultural immersion will be more limited but staying somewhere that caters specifically to children can be a really good way to dip your toes into parts of the world that might otherwise feel out of your comfort zone while removing some of the planning stress.

Despite having travelled independently all our adult lives and having extensive experience of travelling in Africa, when we decided to take our three children to Namibia for two weeks we blew the budget and booked through a specialist operator. This turned out to be the best decision. Not only did the operator locate excellent family-friendly hotels and organise our hire-car and transfers but they worked around difficulties to create a route which allowed us to do everything we wanted. This culminated in five days with a local guide who took us al fresco camping in the Namib desert and taught us all about desert life and Namibia in general. He was such a hit with the kids that our daughter cried when we left him.

**Imogen and Tom Hall,
Lonely Planet**

Handling health and access issues

Family travel is all about the challenge of balancing the different needs of the whole family group. For some families, those needs can be more complex, and as a result trips can be more complicated. Good planning and careful preparation are key – and keeping in mind what an incredible experience you are giving your child makes all the hard work worthwhile.

If your child has particular medical needs, talk to your doctor before you go and make sure your travel insurer is fully aware of your child's preexisting medical condition and that they will cover the loss of any medical supplies and repairs to mobility equipment. If you're flying or taking a train or ferry, make sure you've checked out how the company helps families travelling with children with a disability. Most airports and airlines now have teams whose job is to aid travellers who need additional help. This can be as simple as enabling a child with autism to get through the queues more quickly or providing information on the easiest route through a terminal with a wheelchair, but they can make all the difference to your family's travel experience. Find the right people to talk to at your airline, ferry or train company and make sure you give them plenty of warning about what your needs are and when you are going to be travelling – and keep communicating with them so they don't forget.

If you're flying with a wheelchair, it's best if you can take it to the cabin door. Make sure before you get to the airport that there is an aisle chair or Eagle Hoist available if you need one. Above all, make sure you remove anything that might be damaged in transit (controller, foot plates, etc.) and take it with you on board before the wheelchair is taken to the hold.

If you're taking a wheelchair or any other mobility aid, make sure you check with your accommodation that they have placed you in a ground-floor room or one that is accessible with a lift or elevator, that you have a bathroom that meets your particular access needs

I truly believe the most important thing about exploring is just getting out there and giving it a go. Travel can look different to everyone and can range from exploring your own backyard or heading interstate to travelling across China or trekking in Nepal. Travelling with a wheelchair user does require more organisation and is less spontaneous, but it also opens up a whole new world as people connect with you on a different level as you explore. It means triple-checking with airlines, getting the right travel insurance and trawling through accommodation website photos to see that the accessible room really is accessible! The only way to know if you can do it is to start researching and book that trip!
**Bronwyn Leeks,
Smiths Holiday Road**

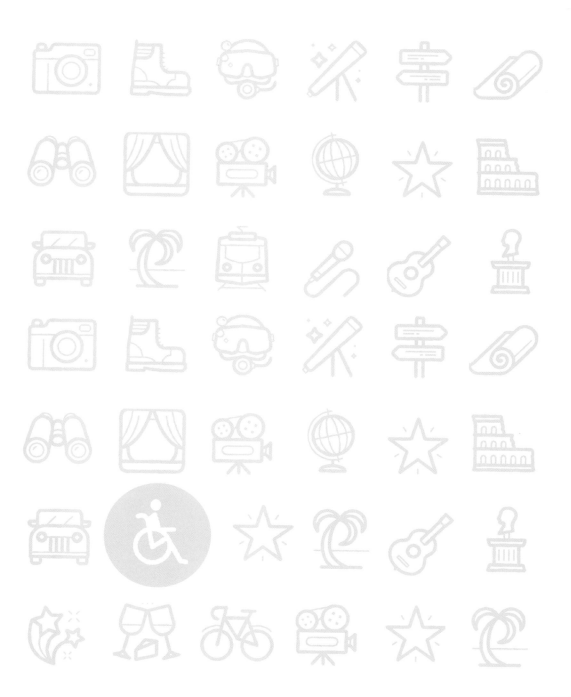

Travelling with a child with anxiety

If your child has anxiety, family travel can be tricky. In order to make it work, you need to think about what an anxious child can cope with, rather than what you'd like to do on holiday. I find that it helps to be calm, and to listen to and accept what an anxious child says about how they're feeling – even if what they say doesn't seem to make sense.

Most UK airports provide (free of charge) a hidden disability lanyard scheme for anyone with anxiety, autism, ADHD or various other conditions. The lanyards signal to staff that the wearer may need extra help or time to go through security, for example. If your child won't wear a lanyard, you can wear it on their behalf.

Gretta Schifano,
Mums Do Travel

don't be afraid to request photographs. It's also wise to check that everywhere you need to go has step-free access. Book taxis in advance or hire cars that have room for not only the wheelchair but everything else you will be carrying (medical equipment and/or continence supplies take up a lot of space). It's also worth researching local tourist offices and organisations that help with special needs to get their insights and advice. You'll find heaps of useful listings for dozens of countries around the world in Lonely

Planet's free Accessible Travel Online Resources. Oh, and make sure the puncture repair kit and a spare inner tube are on your packing list if you're taking a manual wheelchair. If you are taking a power wheelchair, it's worth researching whether there is a local repairer if something goes wrong – and that your charger works with the local voltage!

If your child has autism, you probably know only too well what you are looking for when you book a trip. Do you need a hotel with a quiet space? Should

---

RESOURCES

Blogs written by families dealing with disabilities:

+ Autism Family Travel
www.autismfamilytravel.com
+ Have Wheelchair Will Travel
www.havewheelchairwilltravel.net
+ Smiths Holiday Road
www.smithsholidayroad.com
+ Special Globe
www.specialglobe.com
+ Special Needs Travel Mom
www.specialneedstravelmom.com

Organisations specialising in accessible holidays:

+ Special Needs Vacation by V
www.vacationbyv.com
+ Disabled Holidays
www.disabledholidays.com
+ Discovery Holidays
www.discoveryholidays.com.au
+ Tryb4uFly
http://tryb4ufly.co.uk
+ Up & Up Travel (specialises in Disney)
www.upanduptravel.com
+ Wheelchair Travel
https://wheelchairtravel.org

Things can sometimes go wrong, you may not get the right assistance, or you may have to wait a while, so I would always travel with an open mind. When travelling by plane I always arrive with plenty of time and check in at the desk so I can talk to someone and I always ask if they have an aisle transfer chair. When planning a trip make sure you research the hotel and where you are going on day trips if you have a schedule. This may mean that you will have to ring each place to see if it's accessible. You can roll up and talk to the employees, as places are now getting better as people start to understand the restrictions of someone in a chair, but I always prefer to check.
Abbie Abbott, an avid traveller and manual wheelchair user

you plan out the itinerary in detail so you can talk through exactly what you are going to be doing (and when) ahead of your trip? Involving older children in the choosing and planning of what you do can be helpful in terms of getting ready for the change. A booklet with photos of where you are going and information about what you can expect to see, hear and taste can prepare your child in advance for the upcoming trip.

Travelling with a child who has severe allergies can be a daunting prospect and it's a good idea to discuss your plans with their doctor first. Going to countries where you can communicate easily and there is a good medical infrastructure is often recommended. Contact your carrier and accommodations to make them aware of the allergies and work out any issues. For example, most airlines no longer serve peanuts, but if they still do is there a designated space on the plane where they are not served?

Getting through airport security with any equipment and safe foods that you are carrying can be challenging, but having everything carefully labelled and a letter from your doctor helps. When boarding transport, wiping down seats or covering them with a blanket can avoid contamination from previous passengers, and travelling in the morning means that the carriers are likely to have been cleaned overnight. Laminated cards in the local language to explain your child's allergy are a great idea, and remember to always carry safe snacks for emergencies. Discuss action

Travel essentials checklist

Whether you are a seasoned family traveller or taking your first flight, it pays to have a checklist of what you need to travel.

CHECK THE PASSPORTS

VISA

TRAVEL INSURANCE

While we all know that our passports need to be valid when we travel, for some countries that will mean having a certain amount of time left before it needs renewing. Children's passports expire more quickly than adult ones, so always check the dates with plenty of time to get it renewed. Always make sure that the names you used to book the trip match those in the passport. Shortened or differing names will often not be accepted by border control.

If you are travelling to a country where you need a visa, your children will too. Applying for a visa can be a complicated affair, and even more so when there are several of you to do it for (that's more people who need their photo taken and more forms to fill in), so don't leave it to the last minute and risk the whole trip. Go directly to the embassy website of the country you are planning to visit for the most up-to-date information on visa requirements.

As well as checking whether you need to renew your travel insurance, double-check what it covers. It needs to cover the whole country (or countries) you will be visiting, as well as any activities you'll be engaging in. Check what can be claimed back and any exclusion clauses. If you need to curtail or cancel the trip due to one member of the family becoming ill or injured, is the whole family covered? Check the fine print in advance and your future self will thank you.

REALLY, *DO* CHECK THOSE PASSPORTS!

➤➤➤ We once arrived in Spain, having boarded a ferry in England 24 hours earlier with no issue, where a Spanish border official pointed out that our son's passport was nearly a year out of date. Luckily for us there was a reciprocal agreement in place which allowed some leeway on children travelling on old passports but we spent a few sweaty moments wondering if we were going to be put on the next ferry back. *Imogen and Tom Hall, Lonely Planet*

DOCUMENTATION

HEALTH

If your children don't share your last name, especially if you are travelling as a solo parent, it is important to check what documents you will need to present and when. Some people swear by travelling with copies of birth or adoption certificates, others suggest carrying a letter from their other parent clarifying that you have permission to travel with the children. In South Africa, for example, a letter from the other parent is mandatory. It might be a pain to have to justify that you can travel with your kids, but the rules exist to safeguard against child trafficking or abduction. Carrying a bit of extra paperwork might just help you sail through immigration controls. Also take copies of any important health records that you might need to either show or use in an emergency. Scanning everything (including passports) and attaching it to an email account you can access anywhere you go will keep this documentation safe on the road.

Even if you're travelling to a place with a well-established medical infrastructure, it's worth getting everyone dental and health check-ups before you go to avoid any worries. The last thing you want to be dealing with while you are away is something that could have been sorted out earlier at home. If you are travelling to somewhere that requires vaccinations, make sure you start looking into this with plenty of time to spare, as some courses can take a few weeks or months (for instance, hepatitis). It's also worth getting an international vaccination card to keep a record (and proof) of what you've all had. Note that some countries will require proof of certain vaccinations (such as yellow fever), so make sure you know what is required before you travel.

If you are travelling to an area with mosquito-borne illnesses, long sleeves and insect repellant are musts. Travel insurance is helpful for any medical incidents abroad.

When we travelled to Namibia we made a decision to have our children aged 9, 7 and 3 take antimalarials. Keeping track of the different dosages they needed was a logistical nightmare at first, but we soon got the hang of it and took to carrying a jar of jam around with us, as a spoonful of sugar really did help the medicine go down in our case. We also took the usual precautions: long sleeves and trousers from dusk through the night, sleeping under mosquito nets, using child-friendly repellent (which we had tested at home) and applying it frequently, suffusing clothing with repellent and making use of plug-ins wherever we could (as this is considered more effective).

Imogen and Tom Hall, Lonely Planet

Family finances

Travelling as a family is inevitably more expensive than travelling on your own. Obviously a major outlay is the cost of getting there and back again, but it's worth remembering that some destinations can be expensive to get to but work out as a pretty good value in terms of accommodation and living costs when you are there. Pre-trip research is key to make sure you know what your big costs and your daily costs will be. Sit down and think through every element of the trip from how realistic it is for your family to make picnics every day to whether you can all share one room and still remain sane.

Big attractions such as major historical sites, water or theme parks and major sporting events can all cost serious money, so it pays (no pun intended) to have a chat as a family and work out what is a priority. Having a daily plan helps keep costs down; just leave some leeway for unexpected costs.

REMEMBER: TIMING IS EVERYTHING

Last-minute deals don't tend to exist during the school holidays, and those that do are usually to undesirable places. If your kids are in school then you'll know their term dates far in advance; use this information to book months or even years ahead, when prices are still relatively low due to the lack of demand. If your kids aren't in school yet or you educate them at home, make the most of travelling outside the peak periods, when costs are lower and crowds fewer.

USE YOUR PARENTING NETWORKS

Baby groups may have kept you sane through the newborn haze – but that collective wisdom extends beyond moral support and nappy- or diaper-changing techniques. Quiz fellow parents about trips they've taken, how much they cost and what they would do differently to save money next time. Likewise in the online world there are plenty of forums, Facebook groups and family travel bloggers ready and willing to give you their budget tips on destinations they have visited.

TAKE YOUR FAMILY FAR FROM THE MADDING CROWD

It's basic economics: the higher the demand, the higher the price. One solution? Get off the beaten track. Avoid tourist hotspots and opt instead for somewhere less trendy or famous; think rural Lazio over Tuscany, Adelaide over Sydney and Maine over California. With a bit of research, you'll find fun things to do with the kids and enjoy the luxury of not having to battle through masses of other people to get an ice cream or a family selfie. Plus, you'll acquire the kudos that comes with being just that bit more adventurous.

CHANGE YOUR FAMILY'S TRAVEL HABITS

Instead of trying to get away every time the kids have a break from school, consider going less frequently but for longer, thereby consolidating the costs of getting away in the first place. If you're able to work remotely, you could travel for months, rather than weeks. Alternatively, consider the much-hyped staycation. Switching off and pretending you are on holiday while exploring your local area can be a fun family challenge. Taking trips to visit and stay with family and friends is also a great way to build bonds for your kids...and have some help entertaining them as well.

FAMILY DISCOUNTS ARE YOUR FRIEND

While you can't necessarily take advantage of big group discounts, there are many little ways families can use the power of numbers. You may be able to get a discount pass for local transport, find family coupons online for the attractions you want to see, and take advantage of marketing campaigns such as kids-go-free weeks for theatres or big exhibitions that don't charge entry for children.

STICK TO THE ESSENTIALS

Anyone trying to save money knows it's those little extras that really add up, and the same applies when you are travelling with kids. Take refillable water bottles, buy ice creams by the pack in a local supermarket and read up on the sites you are visiting before you go to avoid paying extra for audio guides, activity packs or special exhibitions. Having an 'eyes only' policy for gift shops can also help keep extra spending at bay.

© COMANICIU DAN / SHUTTERSTOCK

© CAVAN IMAGES / GETTY IMAGES

MAKE THE JOURNEY AN ADVENTURE

Save money on a night's accommodation and create memories you will all treasure by travelling to your destination (or between two points on your itinerary) in a different way. Taking an overnight train or ferry (or even bus if you're brave enough) is a huge event for kids and a story they will retell again and again when back home. Alternatively, a family road trip using your own vehicle avoids the cost of hefty airfares and rental cars.

ENJOY OTHER PEOPLE'S TOYS

While staying in a hotel certainly removes the strain of cooking and cleaning, self-catering using sites such as HomeAway, Love Home Swap or Airbnb is often a much more cost-effective option for families. Renting a house or apartment also provides more space for those who need it (teens in particular welcome extra privacy). You can often find places with toys, games, high chairs or whatever else your family may need. Youth hostels with family rooms are also a more affordable alternative to hotels and will introduce kids to other travellers.

EMBRACE THE GREAT OUTDOORS

Kids thrive in the fresh air, which is great news for budget-conscious parents. Plan day trips that involve nature walks rather than expensive attractions; find the local playground so your little ones can meet other children; and take a picnic to avoid restaurant prices. Another great way to save money while exploring the great outdoors is to camp. It allows kids to be truly immersed in nature while also getting involved with some basic chores (such as post-BBQ clean up), so it's a win-win really – and worth trying at least once, even if you think you won't like it.

Packing list

Some families swear by a laminated packing list which they reuse each time, others prefer to collect things up gradually in the week before and still others function best with a mental checklist. We're certainly not going to spell out for you that you need wipes for the baby, spare clothes for the toddler and everyone else's toothbrush. However, over the years of travelling we have learnt that it is helpful to think about packing in terms of the below criteria.

YOUR CARRY-ON OR DAY SACK

Apart from the essentials such as tickets, passports, wallet and phone, bring whatever else you need in your carry-on to survive the journey. Bear in mind the possibility of any unexpected delays or travel incidents involving bodily fluid, as well as the chance of delayed baggage that doesn't arrive with you. A change of clothes for littles is helpful!

EMERGENCIES

What do you need in case of a medical emergency and where are you going to keep this pack? There's no use having a fantastic medical kit back at the hotel if your youngest takes a nasty tumble on a cobbled street. Make sure you are also carrying your insurance details and local emergency numbers. And while it may not constitute a major emergency, we all know the impact of a hungry child so secret snacks can be their own lifesaver when blood sugar levels are running low. On a similar note, more and more of us use mobile tickets, keep our insurance details in our phone and so on, so remembering a charger (and adapter) can be key for dealing with an emergency.

THE WEATHER

What's the weather going to be like and what are you planning to do? Layers are always good, but even more so with kids, who get hot and cold so quickly. Travelling to a colder climate involves a whole heap of gear you might not use that often where you live. Make sure you have a dry run where everyone tries on their base layers, hats and gloves and wears them for a while. If you are going somewhere warm but you're planning lots of activities, bring clothes that are lightweight and wick away sweat.

WHO IS CARRYING WHAT?

Are your children now big enough to carry their own day packs, and if so what are you going to let them put in them? We're all for fostering independence by letting them make their own choices, but you do need to check that they aren't so weighted down with their dollies or Star Wars ships that they can't fit in the essentials or carry the bag themselves. Also, invariably you don't need as many clothes as you think you do. After you write your list or pack your bag, go away, come back to it, remove 20% and then stick to it. You will be glad you did when you are lugging everything around (including a child) during the trip.

Did somebody say 'overpacking'?

We took our daughter on her first long-haul trip just after her fourth birthday. My husband and I were really looking forward to a three-week tour of New York City and Cape Cod, but our daughter wasn't so keen. She was very sad about leaving our cats at home, and when I started packing for the trip she was adamant that if the cats couldn't travel with us, then some of her favourite toys would have to come along instead. And so it was that we arrived in New York with a large suitcase devoted to our daughter's life-size Baby Born doll and accessories, including a Baby Born collapsible pushchair.
**Gretta Schifano,
Mums Do Travel**

PACKING CUBES

Packing cubes are a family's best friend. They allow you to keep everyone's clothes organised and separate within luggage, and help with keeping dirty items away from the clean stuff.

DEALING WITH BOREDOM

Lastly, put some thought into what you bring to keep different members of the family entertained through any long delay. Sometimes a trip is a great opportunity to introduce a new game, but don't waste valuable space unless you are sure it is going to be a hit. You want to take things you know you and your kids are going to like. Pens and paper are a fail-safe, as are games such as cards, Uno or Dobble. Tablets (with chargers) and a set or two of headphones have saved many a parent from their own meltdown mid-flight, and a Kindle packed with lots of different books can work really well for the young (or old, for that matter) bookworm.

LEARN AS YOU GO

It's the law that the first time you take your baby away you attempt to take everything including the kitchen sink but you still forget some item that turns out to be essential. Go with it, it's all part of the experience – and you won't do it again.

MEDICAL CHECKLIST

The following medications are probably all in your first aid kit at home but it pays to carry them with you when you travel too:

★ Pain relief medicine (child appropriate)
★ Travel-sickness prevention (child appropriate)
★ Saline solution in single doses
★ Cream for burns
★ Arnica cream or granules, plus instant ice packs
★ Anti-nausea treatment (child appropriate)
★ Diarrhea treatment (child appropriate)
★ Oral rehydration solution (child appropriate)
★ Eye drops
★ Antihistamine medicine (child appropriate)
★ Insect bite cream (child appropriate)
★ Antifungal cream to treat infections
★ Antiworm medicine

You will also need some basic medical equipment such as bandages, a shatter-proof children's thermometer and scissors, nail clippers and tweezers. It's also worth including sterile compresses and a good disinfectant and antiseptic lotion. If you are going off the beaten track you will need to supplement your kit with water-purification tablets, syringes and so on. It can be useful to carry anti-worm medicine, and some parents also swear by carrying an anti-fungal cream as a quick way to treat fungal infections, while anti-rash cream tends to be a useful addition.

Wherever you travel, one of the most effective ways to prevent low-level tummy bugs and other illnesses is to be fastidious about washing your hands. Always carry sanitizer gel and make sure everyone uses it frequently. Children tend to touch things more and also to touch their mouth more, so reducing the risk of bacteria transferring from hands to mouth is a good idea.

Get the kids involved

Especially as children get older, involving them in the planning and decision-making before a trip is key to making sure the whole thing runs smoothly and everyone is happy.

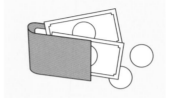

HOLD A FAMILY CONFERENCE

BUDGETING

PACKING

Ask each person to suggest two places they would like to go and why. Does your child have a particular interest – science, the Greek myths, Harry Potter – and could/should you theme a trip around it?

Once you know where you want to go, older kids can help you work out a budget and make suggestions for how you can keep to it. They can also contribute ideas for how the family can save to make the holiday happen and could even do odd jobs or hold a garage sale to make their own donation to the family fund.

Children of all ages can pack their own bags. If you want to make sure that the right things are being included, ask older ones to write out their lists and create a photographic one for younger family members. Get them to think about what they might need to while away the time on a long journey. Giving them independence and respecting their choices allows them to feel responsibility for their belongings.

HEALTH

If a child has special medical needs and you think they are ready, work with them on what they need to carry, what is the best way to do so and where any essential documents should be kept. All children can get involved in putting together the family first aid kit.

PLAYLIST

When preparing for a long journey in the car, ask the kids to create their own playlist for you all to listen to and to give you a list of audiobooks they'd like to hear. For long flights or journeys, downloading their favourite movies or shows to a tablet can also be a lifesaver.

SUSTAINABLITY

If your kids are eco-conscious, let them help find direct flights or plan out a trip by rail or bike. Maybe they even have ideas for volunteering to maintain a trail or work with sea turtles. Kids can also be in charge of refilling reusable water bottles.

Getting there and away

The actual getting there of travel can be the most stressful element of a trip, even if you don't have kids in tow. Add small people with a low boredom threshold, a still-developing awareness of social cues and a tendency to travel sickness, and you've got a heady cocktail of reasons not to venture outside your house in the first place.

The first step is to think it through and plan carefully. But it's also important not to forget the role your own mindset plays. If you start the journey feeling anxious, get progressively more stressed as you hit the small (or large!) hurdles that travelling often throws our way, and end up one big hyperventilating ball of worries, then it's no fun for anyone. And children are very quick to pick up on how the adults in their life are feeling. Dealing with your own stress helps you and them deal better with theirs.

©MICHAEL HITOSHI / GETTY IMAGES

OUR TIPS FOR KEEPING CALM

★
Pack well ahead of time and have a list of things you need to do before you leave the house, thereby reducing the stress of suddenly remembering something essential. Relying on our brains to remember every single thing a family needs to do before you leave for a trip is likely to lead to lapses and oversights.

★
Leave enough time. Moving through an airport or station in a group of people of mixed ages is more complicated than when you are on your own. Add extra time for that unplanned toilet break and you will breathe more easily.

★
Teach yourself breathing techniques (in for three, hold for four, out for five, for example) to help keep your mind and body calm in stressful situations.

★
Always plan for the unexpected, whether it's delays, illness, a lost suitcase or worse. Knowing you have a plan for when something goes wrong can help you deal with anxiety about it happening. Ask your kids what they would do if they got separated from you and discuss ideas together.

★
Don't worry about what other passengers or passersby are thinking. Most likely they are not even thinking about you at all!

★
The getting-from-A-to-B aspect of travel is inherently stressful, but by understanding your own trigger points and practising the art of making the journey fun you can get through it, and even enjoy it.

★
Remember that different ways of getting there suit different temperaments. Is the plane the only option, or would a fun rail or road trip make more sense? Would your child thrive on the security of a cruise or would they rather use their energy on a cycling trip?

Take to the skies

Whether you love to jump on a plane, just about tolerate it because it gets you somewhere you want to be fast, or have a developing phobia of turbulence, flying can be a stressful experience with kids. It starts with the airport, where you have to manage a considerable amount of waiting (whether in a queue for check-in, security or breakfast, or at the gate before you board), and continues on board. The days of sitting back with a glass of wine, a movie you've been meaning to watch for ages and the eye mask ready for when you fall asleep may, to be honest, seem a long way away if you have young children. With kids along, those hours passing through an airport and on an airplane require your best game face, oodles of patience and the ability to grow an extra layer of skin to shield you from the evil stares of the grump across the aisle.

In fact, dealing with other passengers is definitely half the battle when flying with kids. If you're lucky you will get a doting couple happy to read to your kids or play airplane peekaboo, or at the very least tolerate the back of their seat being kicked

© CAIAIMAGE/AGNIESZKA OLEK / GETTY IMAGES

OUR TIPS FOR A SUCCESSFUL FLIGHT

★
Your packing list for your carry-on is as important as those for your checked bags. Be prepared for going through security with everything in zip lock bags and your children briefed that their favourite toy will have to go through the scanner.

★
Little ears can find take-off and landing very hard. Pack gum or something that they can suck on to help with the pressure. If you are nursing, try to nurse at these times.

★
Planes are dehydrating. Make sure you have plenty of water (milk for younger children) and always ask for more.

★
If it's a long-haul flight make sure the tablets are charged, the headphones ready and the shows downloaded.

★
Planes can be dirty and kids like to put their hands to their mouth. Pack and use hand sanitisers.

★
Make sure you've packed enough essentials in your carry-on to see you all through lost luggage or a significant delay.

without turning round and tutting too much. You do however need to be prepared if you are seated next to that one person in the whole plane who absolutely agrees with the concept of kid-free air travel. If this happens to you, remind yourself of the three golden rules: consideration goes both ways (keeping a close eye on your kids to ensure that they are not smearing cake over their neighbour's sleeve or whacking the seat in front of them every five minutes will pay dividends), keep smiling (even the grumpiest person finds it hard to argue with someone being smiley and courteous) and remind yourself that they too were a kid once and it's unlikely that they never travelled.

The other half of the battle is, as always, being prepared. Research the airport and find out if they have security lanes or special boarding gates for families, playrooms or dedicated rest areas for kids, or a system of strollers you can use if you've had to check yours. If your child struggles with the overstimulation of an airport or uses a wheelchair, airports should be able to help you; tell them ahead of time.

★
Zip lock or plastic bags are super useful both to keep things organised and in an emergency.

★
Encourage everyone to walk around a bit at some point to get the blood flowing and improve the mood.

★
Check the rules: you don't want to end up at the gate with a car seat you can't use, going through security with milk you have to chuck away or not being able to use a bassinet when you've planned to.

★
Remember that all flights are time-limited; even bad ones will end eventually! Colouring books or paper for drawing can help the time pass if the onboard entertainment is lacking or batteries don't last the entire trip.

★
Make sure everyone is dressed comfortably, including your teen who has just discovered skinny jeans and heels.

© SSGUY / SHUTTERSTOCK

so it pays to do your research thoroughly and always talk to your doctor or paediatrician before embarking on this route.

Try to give your kids healthy snacks: avoid too much sugar or salt, which can make kids hyper, sick or temperamental. But relax your screen time rules and bring their headphones from home. As your kids get beyond the toddler stage, revel in the fact they will happily watch TV for hours. Whether you let them loose on the technology as soon as you board or save it for when they get really fed up, it's a lifesaver.

If you're travelling with a toddler long haul, book a night flight (or one that works with nap times), grit your teeth and remind yourself frequently that it's only a matter of time until you arrive. The stage where a child wants to move around constantly and has a limited attention span is definitely a challenge on a plane. Seasoned travellers use all sorts of techniques, from wrapping little presents (which can then be opened hourly), wearing the little one out in the indoor play area before they board, and walking up and down the aisle when the cabin crew aren't serving drinks or food.

It's also a wise investment to buy a seat for them even if you technically don't have to. Keeping a wriggling toddler on

If you are going long haul, think about what to take on board that will help your children sleep. Airlines will provide bassinets for little babies, but you will need to request them and also make sure your baby will fit happily inside them. Many people swear by the inflatable cushions you can use to make a proper bed for smaller children (although you do have to remember to ensure their seatbelts are always fastened). Likewise their cuddly or blankie that provides comfort will help them settle in the unfamiliar surroundings. If you are travelling with an infant, make the most of the fact that they sleep a lot and are small enough to keep snuggled in a baby carrier strapped to you. If you are really worried about getting your kids to sleep, there are some over-the-counter medications available. There are many different opinions on this, your lap for any length of time is not anyone's idea of fun. At the same time, remember that even the worst flight will eventually land, and that every fellow passenger was once a screaming child themselves, whether they remember or not. Don't forget that your tantruming toddler is just learning how to travel.

Lastly, don't forget to ask the cabin crew for help. Most of the time they are only too happy to oblige. After all, it's their job to keep the passengers as happy as they can – and happy parents make for happy kids and that makes for a happy plane, making plane crews an excellent last-ditch resort when you're at your wits' end and need assistance.

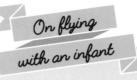

On flying with an infant

Flying with your infant is like the contact sport of parenting. You feel like you have to plan, train, know all the rules and then proceed through the airport dodging people, both well-meaning and mean-mannered, not to mention the stress of boarding, getting yourself situated and wondering if you can keep your baby and yourself comfortably happy for the next two to six (or more) hours all the while praying you don't disturb the entire plane and can endure the death stares of your fellow passengers. **Sarah Stocking, Lonely Planet Destination Editor**

© ALAIN M. DUZANT / 500PX

© YAOINLOVE / SHUTTERSTOCK

RESOURCES

www.flyingwithababy.com is a family travel site written by blogger Carrie, who has 12 years' experience as a long-haul flight attendant

www.seatguru.com has information on airline seat

maps and inflight amenities

www.skyscanner.com is a flight comparison website that will show you the best deals and help you plan how flight times will work with your children's routines

Embrace the open road

Those of us who are lucky enough to own their own car know how much easier it can be to shove the kids, all the luggage and the kitchen sink in the back and head off into the great unknown. You can go at your own pace, stop when you need to and have unlimited freedom to move around when you arrive at your destination. Plus there's music and audiobooks, and now it's easy to connect your tablets to the sound system to keep the kids entertained.

That said, travelling by car is the least environmentally friendly option, statistically it's the least safe and trains and planes can have a special magnetism for little kids.

IT'S ALL IN THE PLANNING

Do your research and find good places to stop en route where legs can be properly stretched and decent fare eaten. Build these into your itinerary; it's worth a detour. Then do the same for wet weather options. Write a list for everything you need for the car (read on to find out what to put on it), assemble said items days ahead to ensure you miss nothing – and make sure these essentials make it to the front seat (and don't get packed away below all your luggage).

BOREDOM BUSTERS

As pilot or copilot on your family's mission to holiday heaven, your role is not simply driver, planner or food provider. You are also entertainer extraordinaire and you need a repertoire of tricks up your sleeve. For younger children, so-called 'old-fashioned' games such as I Spy, Guess the Animal and 'what do the letters on a number or license plate stand for?' all work well. Older children enjoy creating and listening to a family playlist, sharing a good audiobook or playing games such as Twenty Questions. A game of who can stay quiet for the longest is always a winner.

EAT, DRINK AND BE MERRY

An army marches on its stomach and so does a family on a road trip. Make yourself a bag just for snacks, fill it and then repeat. Imagine your worst-case scenario: the world's biggest traffic jam, inclement weather, a breakdown. It's all much more manageable if no one is about to pass out. However, while sweets and chocolate definitely have an important role to play on a long trip with children, healthier alternatives are better for avoiding sugar rushes, dirty hands, travel sickness and the dreaded words 'I'm still hungry' two minutes after eating.

© CATHERINE DELAHAYE / GETTY IMAGES

CHECKLIST

★ If renting a car, car seats pre-booked
★ Tyres, air, fuel all checked
★ Motion sickness pills dispensed, plastic bags at the ready
★ Route planned and plugged in
★ Technology charged
★ Road trip snacks purchased
★ Parental brains engaged for games
★ Parental patience switched to 'ON'

ARE WE NEARLY THERE YET?

The question parents dread to hear, especially as it usually arrives way way way too early for anyone's sanity. The key to handling this is forward planning. Print out your route, mark your stops, get the children to map your progress and answer their own question. For smaller people, explaining the digital clock and how the changing numbers relate to your arrival at your destination can be a good approach.

EMBRACE TECHNOLOGY

Now is not the time to enforce a digital ban, so think before you threaten restricted tablet time as a punishment. Then, make sure everything is downloaded and ready to use, that you have the chargers (and in-car adapters) and that the screens are in a good position (children shouldn't be looking down at them). Lastly, don't resort to the iNanny too soon; there can be too much of a good thing.

Playlist tips

A family rendition (or 100) of Disney's 'It's A Small World' still features in all of our road trips, with the kids' voices going from squeak to growl over the years. Tweens might like Rihanna's 'Shut Up and Drive', while Springsteen's 'Born to Run', or 'Born to Be Wild' might (for better or worse) get Dad singing. We find anything by Queen works; if they're happy in the back then turn up 'Don't Stop Me Now' and if it's all going pear-shaped then 'Bicycle Race' might be more appropriate. 'Hit the Road Jack' and '(Get Your Kicks On) Route 66' are, of course, essential.
Kirstie Pelling, The Family Adventure Project

RESOURCES

Your national automobile association (such as the AAA in the States or the AA in the UK) is a good place to start for advice on driving long distances with kids in the car.

Let the train take the strain

Can you keep the romance of train travel alive when you do it with children in tow? We certainly think so. Not only is travelling by train often cheaper, easier and more environmentally friendly than flying, it's also way more fun for kids. You can move around, there's plenty to look at and the buffet car provides a great distraction.

If you're thinking about taking your kids on a rail adventure, here are five tips to ensure the experience runs smoothly.

PLAN YOUR ROUTE

Travelling by train with kids requires some military-style planning. Start by working out where you want to go and then drill right down to the smallest detail so you know the durations, the stations and all the changes involved.

Consider how long you think you and your kids can survive on one train without changing. Three hours is a good starting point for a family with younger children. Try to minimise the number of times you have to transfer and avoid connections that will be hard to make if you have a sudden meltdown or nappy change to deal with. Book in advance with reserved seats to make sure you can all sit together (and to save money). If possible, avoid rush hour, busy routes and big events. Naturally school holidays are crunch points. Investing in a local family discount card or a rail pass where kids under 16 travel for free or at a discounted fare can be very cost effective.

© SANDRA SAMUELSSON / GETTY IMAGES

RESEARCH FAMILY-FRIENDLY OPTIONS

Across the world there's huge variety in terms of what 'family-friendly' means. In Italy your children will be fussed over by fellow train travellers but you might struggle to find baby changing facilities, whereas in Finland your children can take advantage of a dedicated playroom on some InterCity trains. Think about what really matters to your family when choosing trains and routes. Does your teen make life a misery when deprived of wi-fi? Do you need to be near the toilet for your preschooler? Does being in a designated family carriage reduce your stress levels?

Most of the main European train companies have an English-language version of their site, so use it to understand what you are booking. In many places there are discounts for children travelling with adults or excellent value rail passes for families.

© PHOTO AND CO / GETTY IMAGES

TRAVEL LIGHT AND ARRIVE EARLY

Travelling light is key to moving around railways easily. Carry only what you can handle together and train your children to take their own hand luggage and think carefully about bringing the buggy or stroller. It can be a lifesaver helping children get to sleep and as a packhorse, but negotiating lots of steps and having to put it up and down all the time can be hard work. If you are at the stage when a stroller is a fact of life, take one that folds up easily and be prepared to stow it away from you. Have a counting system to make sure you get everyone and everything on and off the trains safely and get to the station with plenty of time to board at the same time. Avoid splitting up: it has been known for one parent to get stuck in another coach for four hours due to a combination of late boarding and no interlinking carriages.

EXPECT THE UNEXPECTED

As usual it pays to be prepared for illness (change of clothes, medicine, wipes), no trolley car or buffet service (snacks, water, more snacks), no seats together (those backpacks that double as car boosters can be impromptu seats for little bottoms) or delays or disruption to the service. It's also worth prepping your children for busy stations and having a plan in case you become separated. Bright colourful clothing and your phone number in their pocket is a good start, as well as showing them what a guard looks like.

Equally, embrace the positive. The locals who go out of their way to help you, the sudden offer of an upgrade to first class, the diversion on the line which takes you on a more picturesque route and makes the kids go 'wow'. It's all part of the amazing adventure of rail travel.

Just don't leave a child behind!

After passing through security in St Pancras International Station we were very pleased to be boarding the train complete with three children, a buggy and what we thought were all our bags. At the last minute we realised we had left our main suitcase at the scanner in the rush to get the buggy off the conveyor belt and locate all the security-cleared children. Luckily there was just enough time to grab it but since then we've always used the counting system.
Imogen and Tom Hall,
Lonely Planet

MAKE IT FUN

Even the most train-obsessed toddler gets bored once the train has been moving for a while. Ideally your family will be seated round a table so make the most of the communal surface and bring plenty of travel games, books, colouring and of course the tablets. Don't forget the charger and headphones.

Having more space makes things easier so, if you can stretch your budget, use the savings made from booking well in advance to go first class. That feeling of being extra special can help with behaviour. There's little more exciting for kids than taking a sleeper train overnight.

FAMILY TRAVEL HANDBOOK

All aboard: Cruising with kids

Cruising is having a moment. The old formula has been tossed overboard in favour of a new style of sailing, from expeditions to the edge of the world to itineraries built around your interests. There's also an increased focus on sustainability, and many operators are now fully aware of the commercial benefits of catering more specifically to families. But is a cruise right for your family? Those in favour sing the virtues of both the onboard entertainment which can keep little ones happy for hours and the fact you can make multiple stops and see a lot of a region while not having to keep unpacking and relocating. Cruises on megaships can also work very well for multigenerational trips, as there are options for every member of the family, the meals are all taken care of and everyone gets their own space in the cabin.

Detractors talk about the impact of being in close proximity to large numbers of your fellow cruisers (if your family needs space and calm, be aware that this is going to be harder to find on a cruise) and the often strict schedules (if you like to make things up as you go when travelling, then the lack of spontaneity could ruin your trip). If getting out daily in the natural world or having a wide-ranging freedom of motion is important for your family, the limitations of being on board might have a negative effect on your enjoyment. There's also the impact on the environment to consider. If your family is very concerned with their footprint, then you need to do your research to be sure taking a cruise is something you will all feel comfortable with.

If you do decide on a family-friendly cruise, there are some handy tips to keep in mind.

Make sure you choose a cruise that caters to children in a meaningful way, not just a babysitter service so grown-ups can hit the casino. These days companies such as Carnival, Celebrity Cruises, Disney and Royal Caribbean offer state-of-the-art ship design with an incredible array of kid-friendly facilities, such as wave pools,

© OLGA GAVRILOVA / SHUTTERSTOCK

rock-climbing walls and movie theatres.

Give careful consideration to the excursions you chose: activities such as snorkelling, hiking and kayaking might hold the kids' attention for longer than guided, sometimes rushed, tours of churches, museums and markets. Likewise, there can be a dizzying array of activities available on ship. Devote some serious time to planning your family's schedule, and avoid anyone feeling overlooked because they haven't managed to do what they wanted to. You may have to pay extra for some options, such as abseiling or cooking, but this can turn out to be a good investment when your teen is fully engaged, having fun and learning a new skill. Alternatively, let kids pick their own preferred activities and roll with a casual, laid-back approach to planning; after all, on a cruise the big stuff is taken care of for you.

Know the rules: different cruises have different age restrictions and different approaches; once again your pre-trip research will help here. You don't want to end up not being able to take your toddler into the swimming pools on a Disney ship because she's not potty trained, for example.

Invest in a few high-quality maps so your children can learn to measure distance, memorise the names of bodies of water and far-flung cities, and keep a captain's log of key geographical features. This may keep them engaged on a different level as you cross the Mediterranean or sail through the Suez Canal.

Be prepared: being so far out to sea can freak out some children, especially during life jacket drills, so talk to them about what to expect and avoid watching *Titanic* the night before boarding. Weak wi-fi signals can also disturb older children, but another fun way to stay in touch is via walkie-talkies. Just check first that you won't be making waves with the ship's crew.

Consider giving each child a small amount of daily pocket money and encourage them to plan and make purchases in the safe and secure environment of a ship's confines.

© GLENN VAN DER KNIJFF / GETTY IMAGES

43

Boarding the bus with kids

Travelling by long-distance bus or coach is usually a cheaper but lengthier option for getting from A to B. There are good discounts for kids and families, so if you need to save money and are ready for the challenge of keeping children entertained on a long journey with limited stops then the bus could be the right option for you. Some carriers have entertainment systems and wi-fi on board, which definitely help pass the time – or travelling at night so everyone sleeps for part of the journey can work. Be aware of the schedule so you know the stops (and also so you can point out where you are); be prepared to hit traffic and get delayed; load up the tablets with both charge and downloads; and if your child gets car sick, stock up on anti-motion sickness pills. Bring a blanket, as some buses can get very cold.

© DUSANPETKOVIC / GETTY IMAGES

© IRINA KLYUCHNIKOVA / SHUTTERSTOCK

Get the kids involved

★ As soon as they are old enough, encourage your kids to think about what they need for the in-transit part of your trip and to pack their own bag (which they can then carry). Not only is this teaching them independence, but it also means they should end up with things they want to read and play with.

★ Whatever method of transport you are taking, spend some time teaching your kids how it works. Find some fascinating facts to wow them with.

★ Get each family member to come up with an easy game to play when you have to pass the time waiting.

★ Be prepared to spend some money at the terminal buying a magazine or new book which the kids choose themselves: you're investing in the journey.

Making the trip run smoothly

You've survived! Maybe you've even followed our advice and actually thrived on the journey to your destination and the whole family has arrived feeling calm, happy and excited to explore a new corner of the world. Right?

In reality the first few hours or days of being in a different location need to be considered the 'relocation zone'. Everyone – including the main carers or adults in your group – needs time to adjust to the new normal: where are we sleeping, eating, using the bathroom; how are we getting about; what are we going to do; what's fun, what's a bit challenging. This applies even if you are going somewhere you've been before. It's all different from home and for little people that can be discombobulating. Allow children time to explore their new location, get to know their rooms and the layout of the hotel or apartment, and, crucially, understand where their parent or parents will be sleeping.

Take some deep breaths and take your time to settle in. Allocate a slow first day, especially if you are dealing with jet lag or have had a long journey. If you're travelling with a partner, divide and conquer so one of you tackles checking-in, getting the rental car, stocking up, finding a nice cafe, whatever it is you need to do, while the other looks after the kids. Prioritise feeding, as everyone feels better and ready to tackle a new challenge when they have something in their stomachs.

It's also worth remembering that just getting everything at

HANDLING JET LAG IN KIDS

⫸⟶ Changing time zones is hard work regardless of how old you are and the same rules for dealing with jet lag apply to kids as to adults. Some families advocate changing infants' and toddlers' schedules gradually as you approach the day of travel, others use natural over-the-counter sleep aids (but research this carefully first to be sure you want to go down this path). If it's only a short trip it's always an option to stay on your schedule from home and not adjust to local time. Otherwise remember to stay hydrated and sated and get the kids out in the fresh air for some sunlight and exercise. If you can keep everyone awake so they go to sleep as near to the new bedtime as possible that's a good start. Whatever you do avoid scheduling too much on your first few days while recovering.

In many cultures around the world it's entirely normal for children to be patted, and hugged and have their hair ruffled by complete strangers. It's a beautiful way to demonstrate to children that they are a treasured part of society, but remember it's always acceptable to say no or ask someone to stop doing what they are doing; just communicate it with respect and in the local language if possible. That handled, travelling to places where children are celebrated is often much more relaxing than visiting countries where children are merely tolerated.

The other side of the coin is that there are still places in the world, for example some areas of Europe, where you may feel that your children are to be seen and not heard when out in public. Focus on finding family-friendly attractions and places to eat if you want to make life a bit easier.

home ready so you can go away and then physically getting everyone to your destination can be mentally stressful and physically tiring for the adults in your party. Pair this stress with the release and perspective that comes from being away from the daily grind and you can see why it's not uncommon for parents and carers to have days during a trip where they feel emotionally exhausted. When this happens be kind to yourself, talk to the rest of your party and maybe even reconfigure your plans for the day.

Looking after yourself is as important as looking after your family. If you are travelling with your partner or in a bigger group, you can build in some 'me time' for the adults by having a couple of days where one person or couple looks after the kids and vice versa. This could allow someone to try a new activity or someone else to wander at leisure around a museum, or a couple in the group to go out for dinner together.

Lastly, keep in mind that travelling as a family is usually a rollercoaster ride. There will be highs, there will be lows, but ultimately it's a thrill which your family will always remember. Your mindset is as important as all your planning. Have fun working out your plans, take opportunities that present themselves, and make the most of every day you are travelling. Try to avoid having rigid expectations and be ready to go with the flow, pivot plans and most of all enjoy the time together exploring the world.

Where to stay

The number and variety of housing options
available for families has boomed in recent years.

Where your family will stay on your travels depends heavily on your changing needs. Thankfully the choices are more plentiful than ever before. Often more expensive than other places to stay, a hotel is a good option if you don't need to cook (and let's face it, having a break from having to think about feeding your family three times a day is definitely part of the reason to have a holiday), want to be somewhere central and generally want to feel like you're doing something a bit special or different. If some of your own childhood memories include splashing in a hotel pool or the excitement of sleeping in a 'posh' room then you will identify with how much children can love being in hotels, though check whether the pool has hours it is off-limits to kids.

The number of hotels that want children to be seen and not heard is in the minority now. Most openly welcome them and many luxury hotels actively cater to families with a variety of activities, playgrounds, children's meals and babysitting services.

Not to mention hotels which are linked directly to theme parks, where the fun is entirely family focused. Families who belong to a loyalty points system may find that they can even get free stays.

On the downside, unless you have a suite or connecting rooms, staying in a hotel usually means being in just one room with each other, which can create issues. Many parents we know have spent time hanging out in a hotel bathroom while the baby sleeps in the space and comfort of the actual room. If

you are booking more than one room be sure to clarify if they are connecting or adjoining (there's a big difference when it comes to little children especially). Having to climb lots of stairs with babies, tired toddlers and all your bags can also be hard work, so check about elevators or prepare yourself for some heavy lifting, unless there are porters or you have made sure to book a ground floor room.

Smaller guest houses offering bed and breakfast can also be a good option for a more personal welcome but check reviews carefully to be sure they like kids, and if so how accommodating they can be of any specific requests you have such as child-friendly meals and extra beds or cots for the room.

HOSTELS

Often and understandably associated with a rowdy backpacker crowd, hostels might not be your first choice for family accommodation, and certainly it's important to do your research and avoid those with a party reputation. However, more and more hostels around the world are offering simple family rooms at affordable prices, allowing you to take advantage of the positives of hostelling (low cost, self-catering, meeting other travellers) while avoiding the delights of sharing a dorm with strangers. Note that children are not normally allowed to sleep in dorms anyway. Family rooms normally come with clean beds, a bathroom and wi-fi; what more do you need? Hostelling International is a good place to start your search for family stays.

FARM STAYS AND AGRITOURISM

Staying on a working farm can be an incredible experience for children, especially those who live in towns or cities. Your children can get involved in feeding the animals and mending fences while learning about nature and farming. Being part of a farming family just for a few days is a real education, and adults often find that immersing themselves in a completely different life to their own provides a proper restorative break. Farm stays can be found online at WWOOF (Worldwide Opportunities on Organic Farms).

CAMPING

If you're a family who embrace the outdoors, then camping is a rewarding and cheap accommodation option. It helps you live a simpler life for a few days, the fresh air encourages you to relax with the family and it is a really interesting way to get to know a destination. Cabin sites, some of which have electricity, are an easy in-between option if carrying all your gear on a flight isn't appealing. Turn to the next chapter, which is dedicated to exploring the great outdoors as a family, for more information and ideas about camping.

UNIQUE STAYS

➤➤➤ Spending the night somewhere really unusual is how childhood memories are made. Why not include one of these experiences into your trip?

- Follow in the movie's footsteps with a night at a museum
- Climb up high and bed down in a treehouse
- Learn about the night sky by sleeping out with fellow stargazers
- Hang out with our furry, feathered or fishy friends with a sleepover at a zoo, aquarium or aviary
- Be rocked to sleep on a night train or drop your anchor aboard a boat
- Step back in time by sleeping in a castle

APARTMENT RENTALS, HOMESTAYS & HOME SWAPS

For families with infants or young children or those travelling in larger groups, a home rental is often an excellent option. Not only do most rentals come with a kitchen to allow for preparing meals during your stay, communal common areas also allow your group more time bonding together. You can even worry less about disturbing other people if you have a baby still waking up in the night or a toddler who rises before the lark.

Of course there are a variety of different options here, from basic apartments often catering to business travellers and located within wider hotel complexes to whole houses that are permanently rented out or personal homes made available on an ad hoc basis. The latter can work especially well for families when home comforts such as high chairs, cots, toys and games are all provided or accessible. Remember to double-check what is provided before you book. It also pays to make sure that you are relatively close to a supermarket or local shops and to know where the nearest child-friendly restaurants are. Sites such as Airbnb, HomeAway or Vrbo are some go-tos for these rentals, though regulations vary by region.

Another option is a home swap where one family stays in another's home for free. Not only is this great value, it's also usually a really fantastic option for experiencing life as a local as your hosts will leave recommendations, often including advice with specific child recommendations. Any worries about safety and damage can be allayed by using a reputable site or exploring any friends-of-friends connections you have.

Right from top: A rooster at Mar Vista Cottages; a Thai homestay family. Above: A Grenada homestay.

© MARK READ / LONELY PLANET

© MATT MUNRO / LONELY PLANET

Where and what to eat

Making sure the little darlings are safely and satisfactorily fed and watered is high on parents' agendas. Add to this the fact that food is a key way to explore and learn about a different culture and what, where and how you are going to eat each day becomes a vital component of your trip. Mealtimes are lovely opportunities to engage with your kids, especially when you are away from the daily stresses of life. Make the time to eat and enjoy local foods together.

Mornings can be the most productive time for families, who are often up early, so make sure you've got breakfast options to get ready for a good day ahead. If you've just arrived in a hotel and everyone is a bit jet lagged, then check what time breakfast finishes and negotiate some flexibility. Or send your partner out to find somewhere good for brunch.

As you are out and about exploring, a stop off for coffee, lunch, ice cream or dinner can be a welcome break as well as an essential refuelling stop. Choose somewhere where quite a few people are eating, ideally locals. If they like it then that's a good sign, and with lots of customers you have less chance of being served yesterday's leftovers. It's worth checking there's something on the menu your kids will eat. Be prepared to be patient while waiting for your food and have cards (or similar) on hand to keep everyone busy while you wait.

Be aware that mealtimes vary from country to country. If your children are old enough to be a bit flexible with their eating habits, doing as the locals do will help you get the most from your experience, but equally being a bit flexible yourself can help. You may want to embrace the local culture and dine late, but if your little one is just not going to make it without a meltdown it pays to rethink your day and make the lunchtime meal your focus. After a busy day, settling down at your accommodation with your own home-cooked meal often works well for kids who can be tired and over-stimulated. Alternatively if you've found a restaurant that you all like and makes your family feel welcome, then stick with it. We're definite fans of trying new things but sometimes the newly familiar is what everyone needs at the end of a day exploring.

Similarly on some days a picnic made from visiting a local shop and putting together something recognisable like a sandwich and snacks can be a good and reassuring alternative to dining out, as well as saving you money. You might even want to pack some of their usual snacks in your suitcase for days when a little taste of home is needed. Emergency cereal bars that you know travel well are winners.

Although you probably want to sample a variety of local dishes, unless you've raised kids with incredibly adventurous palates the chances are that your younger children might not be so keen on trying food that they don't recognise. Rest assured that almost anywhere in the world you can get hold of the basic foodstuffs: rice/potatoes, vegetables, fruit and so on. It's worth taking your lead from your kids – if they want to try something new encourage them but don't force it if they don't want to. For a short trip it's really not going to cause issues if their diet is a little less varied than usual, and familiar foods will provide comfort to kids in a new environment.

Right: Local foods can sometimes tempt adventurous eaters, but there's always ice cream when all else fails.

Staying healthy

Making sure your kids are hydrated, particularly if you are travelling in a hot country, helps with hunger pangs and energy levels and generally keeps them healthy. Remember children are more prone to

Above: A classic summer or holiday treat. Right: Trying xiaolongbao (soup dumplings) at a Taiwanese night market.

© SIVAN ASKAYO / LONELY PLANET

dehydration than adults. Keep the water coming and avoid too many sugary drinks (this includes drinks like apple tea in Turkey) which can make you more thirsty. It's common sense but make sure you are clear on whether the water is safe to drink, and if in doubt make sure it's boiled for five minutes before drinking, or else swallow your sustainable principles and buy bottled drinking water. Avoiding ice may also be best if there are concerns about the water. And remember that if you're travelling with someone with allergies it is a good idea to have laminated cards with pictures and information on the allergy in the local language made before you depart.

When it comes to food and drink, make sure you've done your research so you know what is safe to consume and what is better avoided, and trust your instincts. But also remember that you are a role model to your children: show them that trying new foods and joining in with the local food culture is a rewarding experience.

And if all else fails, remember that ice cream (provided it's safe to eat and not outrageously expensive) is usually a fail-safe route to happy, contented kids and adults. Always always always have spare change and an eye out for the nearest place to find the cool creamy stuff. It's what family holidays are made of.

© IPPEI NAOI / GETTY IMAGES

FOOD HYGIENE TIPS

If you are travelling beyond Europe and North America, it's worth getting your kids to understand the basic hygiene rules. After all, you're setting them up for a lifetime of hopefully good travel strategies:

★
Make sure hands are properly clean before you eat; always carry hand-sanitising gel and use it often, and always wash hands before eating.

★
Aim for fruit that you peel yourself: bananas are usually a good bet.

★
Avoid salad, raw vegetables, pre-peeled fruit – or anything that might have been washed in water.

★
Avoid cold pre-cooked or raw meat.

©TINA GARCIA / LONELY PLANET

★
Be wary of ice cream in areas where power goes on and off.

★
Steer clear of shellfish and only eat fish that has been cooked and is the normal fare in the region.

★
Milk should be boiled and fresh cheese or yoghurts avoided.

★
Fruit juices or anything that could have water added to it or components that could have been washed in water should be avoided.

Travelling at every age

In the interests of holiday harmony it is worth bearing in mind the needs of individuals within your group. If you are travelling with an infant you are already tuned to their feeding, sleeping and safety needs. Older children might be more independent and able to care for themselves, but it's worth spending some time thinking about what they too need to keep them safe and happy while you are away. This could be as simple as a reminder about how to make safe choices about what you eat and drink, how to think about traffic and what to

© MAICA / GETTY IMAGES

© TINA GARCIA / LONELY PLANET

HOW TO TRAVEL WELL WITH AN INFANT

★
Make a list of what you need before you go and then use it to ensure you don't forget anything essential.

★
If you are travelling by air or have to go through any security screenings, then know what the latest rules are in terms of liquid and food so you don't have to deal with the stress of losing anything.

★
Carry formula or pumped milk or familiar food from home. There is usually a way to improvise, but having something you know they will eat with you makes life easier.

★
Consider bringing your own car seat, as this can cut down on the inevitable stress of having to work out how to install the rental one, plus you can often use it on the plane to help the little one sleep.

INFAnts

⫸⟶ Parenting your first baby is an overwhelming experience and your first trip away with them can be somewhat of an endurance test as you learn how to navigate a new world with the tiniest most precious bundle (and usually everything from your home except the kitchen sink) in tow. By the time you get to subsequent children you realise that actually traveling with an infant is surprisingly easy and you begin to wish you'd done more trips when you just had one child. Embrace the fact that the baby sleeps much of the time, can be carried in a sling, wrap or carrier easily and is usually pretty easily satisfied as long as they have food and comfort. Remember you know your baby best and before the trip have a good think about how best to handle the different stress points of the day.

take into consideration when weighing up a potentially risky physical activity. However, it's important to think about emotional needs too. Involving children in the planning and decisions about where to go and what to do kickstarts their investment in a trip. Letting them bring their phone, plenty of books, a specific game or whatever it is they like to do to relax shows that you know their involvement, engagement and downtime is important.

Likewise if you are travelling as part of a multigenerational group, you might need to put some extra groundwork in on your daily itinerary before you go, starting with creating a list of all the things that are key for individuals to enjoy themselves. In a perfect world we would all be wonderfully flexible and just go with the flow, but in reality, and especially when we're taking a well-deserved break, most of us want or need specific things to really enjoy ourselves. Making sure Grandpa gets his postprandial nap, Auntie Vi gets to visit the museum she's always wanted to go to and the little kids have some outdoor space to run off steam will pay dividends when you get to the end of the day and everyone has a big smile on their face.

★
Noise-cancelling headphones can be a useful way to help infants nap.

★
Be prepared to change nappies/diapers everywhere and anywhere; likewise it's worth being flexible about where you are happy to breastfeed.

★
Enjoy it when people comment on your baby, and smile and engage with him or her. This is your first experience of how travelling with kids opens doors you never knew about.

Toddlers

© TANG MING TUNG / GETTY IMAGES

Do you find sitting still is highly overrated? Do you have the patience to engage a living being with a very short attention span for a relatively long period of time out of the home? Are you skilled in deciphering communication that is half verbal and half nonverbal? Is your speciality dealing with fist-pumping, red-faced screaming little people without losing your own cool? If the answer is yes to all the above then you are ready for the toddler travel challenge! The toddler years pass in a flash, but those memories of your sweet pint-sized human exploring a new place will stay with you forever.

SURVIVAL TIPS FOR TRAVELLING WITH A TODDLER

★	★	★
Book trains, sites and attractions for early in the day where possible so you are active when energy levels are highest.	Start with visits to family and friends who can help keep your child entertained while out and about (and who know all the insider tips of their location).	If your child is still napping be sure to work around the naptime (and make the most of it for yourself too).
★	★	★
Take regular breaks from sightseeing on your trip to run off steam and generally keep everyone sane. You don't have to see and do everything!	Don't feel pressured into boarding planes early – if you are travelling with others, you can divide and conquer by sending someone ahead to get your seats set up and having someone else stay in the terminal with the toddling ball of energy and attempting to wear them out.	Jet lag with a toddler is evil. Embrace being up in the middle of night, work out a plan for adjusting their naptimes slowly and just go with it. Seriously, you can't make it go away and you can't get a toddler who thinks they should be awake to go to sleep, so don't try.
★	★	★
On long trips having 'surprises' up your sleeve can work well to keep toddlers entertained.	Find places to explore that are toddler tolerant – for example, large sites with plenty of space to run around in the fresh air.	Pack familiar snacks, books and comforts to provide reassurance away from home.

★ Travelling with a toddler who is learning how to use the toilet can be hard work. If you're not already using one, a portable potty is a useful addition to your luggage at this stage. Plus, bring along the usual changes of clothes and a positive attitude from the parents. Kids will have accidents and it's rarely the end of the world when they do, so smile and focus on how nice it is not to have to change nappies.

★ Remember it's a blessing to be able to be out and about exploring the world with your nearest and dearest. The challenges are to be navigated together!

★ Adjust your expectations: it's perfectly possible to take a toddler to a world-famous gallery, but you won't be there for hours.

★ Kids museums are perfect spots to take your toddler for age-appropriate fun; balance them out with adult sites.

★ If you aren't planning to home educate, make the most of the opportunity now to take your kids away outside of school holidays. You will miss the freedom once they are in the school system.

★ Keep calm and smile: your little person picks up quickly on stress, so manage theirs and yours by keeping a positive outlook. This also helps when dealing with other people who are far more likely to be helpful and understanding if you look happy.

★ Prepare your child for the next day the night before so they can get adjusted for a new environment or activity.

The milk train in India

'Milk please, Mummy'. Three words you never want to hear at 3am, especially when you're wedged onto the top bunk of a sleeper train. During the incredible year we spent living and travelling in India, the late-night milk run was always tricky – climb down from bed, find thermos flask, half hot water, half cold, milk powder, shake and pass to child. Two minutes later he'd curl up into my arms and drift back to sleep. With another parenting challenge passed, I'd drift off too, happy in the knowledge we'd soon be waking in a new Indian city to explore as a family.
Jenny Lynn,
Travelynn Family

Elementary & primary school

In many ways this is the best age for travelling with kids. You've left the very small person stage behind and with it the need to lug nappies, buggies and 50 changes of clothes around with you, and you now enjoy the freedom of no longer being chained to a nap schedule. This is also the point where children are starting school and learning more and more about the world. The broadening of horizons in the classroom often translates to an enthusiasm for learning about wherever they are. Now is the time to capitalise on trips that link to what they are learning at school: often the Aztecs, the Egyptians or the Greeks may feature. Find books that tell stories or give information on what they are interested in, talk to them about your trip in advance and get them drawing or writing or photographing their experiences. You will treasure these mementos later.

THE FOLLOWING CAN BE USEFUL WHEN TRAVELLING WITH A SCHOOL-AGE CHILD

★ Activities: books, sketchpad and pencils, journal

★ Binoculars: to zoom in on wildlife, details of buildings or just their siblings

★ Pocket camera: they will learn a new skill that keeps them engaged, and they may turn out to be better than you at photography

★ Fold-away scooters and/or rollerblades: useful if you are covering longer distances on foot

★ Their own daypack: to carry all the above

★ A tennis ball: turns any green space into a ball field and opens doors with local kids

★ Pack of cards: turns any wait into some fun

★ Water bottle: they are never too young to learn about avoiding single-use plastic

★ Snacks: just, snacks

★ Snorkel and mask: if you are going to be spending any time in water

★ Bucket, spade and kite: for the beach

Tweens

© PETER CADE / GETTY IMAGES

Children between eight and 12 years old are very much still kids but they're also experiencing hormonal changes as they prepare for teenage life. Parenting and travelling with this age of child is no less challenging than any other. You have to be prepared for them to be exuberantly childlike one minute and a monosyllabic teen the next. Try to be as flexible and as understanding as you can, treating them as responsible young people while continuing to be patient. Consult them on plans. Build in any small opportunities for independence.

Let them pack their own bags, manage their own spending money, and perhaps even lead the whole family for a day. Plan for them to have lazy days when you get up late, and don't cram too much in, so they can recharge emotionally and physically. And when they revert to being little kids, if you possibly can drop everything, give them your undivided attention and make the most of every minute of it.

Teens

We're not going to beat about the bush: travelling with teenagers can be hard work. They may be reluctant to take holidays with their families (preferring time at home with friends), leading to them being less than engaged while away. You may mourn the holidays where your children hung onto your every word and were utterly fascinated by the world you were showing them, but that child is still in there and with a little careful persuasion you can get them to come out again. Travelling with your teen can be a good way to reconnect with them, so rather than avoid the trip, plan it with them in mind.

HOW TO MAKE YOUR HOLIDAY TEEN-FRIENDLY

★

Think about what your teenager really loves to do and factor that into the plans, whether it's watching rugby, taking part in something active like mountain biking or climbing, or a trip to an art gallery.

★

It can be hard being away from your friends as a teenager. Would a shorter trip work better at this point?

★

Does your teen respond to one-on-one time, making this a good point to arrange a trip that doesn't involve siblings or wider family?

★

A walking tour with a specific theme can be a good way to get a teen excited about a place, especially if you can build in some fun elements like quirky transport (think Segways!) or plenty of selfie opportunities. The unique is exciting for the teen brain, not to mention the brag factor.

★

Feeling independent is key. Go somewhere that you know will be safe for your teen to take off on their own for a bit. Even better if you can find activities that they can do on their own for a day or two.

Travelling with teenagers

Each of my kids has refused to come on a family holiday at some point during their teenage years – but we've always worked something out and they've come along in the end. If your teen wants to opt out of a family trip, but they're too young to stay at home alone, you either have to persuade them to come along, or you need to find a kind adult to look after them while you're away. My key teen travel-persuasion strategies are to involve them as much as possible in family holiday planning, and also to make sure that trips include things which they really enjoy, such as football stadium tours for my son, and exploring local markets for my daughter.
Gretta Schifano,
Mums Do Travel

★

A digital detox is a lovely idea in principle, but if your teen is going to hate it and the whole trip as a result then make sure you have wi-fi. Open the discussion before you go – they might actually welcome a break from the internet and everything it brings with it, too.

★

If you are bringing the tech gadgets, find some good local apps to support your teenager's emotional investment in the trip. A basic language one is a good start but anything that helps them find a fun place for a coffee, a trendy gallery to visit or an unusual activity to try out helps.

Tips for travelling with a solo child

Travelling with only one child can be challenging. All relationships are put to the test when on the road, and the unique dynamic of 'only child' families – one in which the child often has to define their place in a world of mostly adults – can find itself even more fraught when tensions arise in a hotel room or an airport lounge. Here are some suggestions to help:

FOSTER THEIR INDEPENDENCE

Kids who grow up without siblings are generally quite precocious for their age, often because they spend so much time in an adult-oriented home. Take advantage of their relative maturity by letting them learn to make their own choices and deal with new situations, cultures and people while travelling. You'll need to decide what's appropriate given their age and the location, of course.

MEET OTHER KIDS

Before you leave, do some research into venues where local kids like to gather, such as nearby playgrounds, amusement parks, day camps, after-school activities or child-friendly festivals that might be on while you're there. Besides staving off their potential feelings of isolation, letting your child meet and play with kids from other cities or countries is a terrific experience that can help them learn a lot about the destination's culture directly from their local counterparts.

Travelling one-on-one

My daughter and I started a tradition of taking annual mother-daughter trips where she has the final say on our choice of destination and I work hard to make sure we have a mix of active, learning and relaxing activities. Travelling one-on-one with your child has its challenges, as you are the sole source of entertainment, as well as the navigator, decision maker and parent. I make sure to involve her in the planning and allow her to choose one 'splurge' activity that she is really excited to try. The benefits of one-on-one travel far outweigh the challenges. The change of environment opens up new opportunities for bonding and conversation. I'm so grateful that my teen still cherishes these trips, to the point that she turned down the offer to bring a friend, so that we could keep it just for the two of us. These memories will be something that we both look back on fondly as she grows up and goes off on her own.
Tamara Gruber, We 3 Travel

SPLIT UP FOR THE DAY

If you're off to a destination with lots of different options, schedule in some 'duo days', where the child can go with one parent at a time to do something more specific to their tastes – while the other parent then has a free day to follow their own pursuits.

BRING ALONG A FRIEND

Let your only child choose a sibling stand-in – ask their best friend's parents if their child can join you on the road. Besides letting you take real advantage of all those 'two adult, two children' family-discount passes, having a friend along will take the pressure off you and your spouse to continually engage with your child – who also gets to have some quality time with a peer. Bringing an older family member like a cousin, who can act as babysitter, is another option.

GIVE THEM THEIR SPACE

Only children grow up learning how to keep themselves occupied and as a result many come to need regular alone time. Don't forget to pack things that your kid can use to get away from the grown-ups for a bit: books or an e-reader, a tablet loaded with music and movies, their own camera or a travel journal.

© KONSTANTIN VORONOV / GETTY IMAGES

Travelling as a solo mum

I never felt different or disadvantaged traveling as a solo mum; in fact I felt empowered and so, so lucky. I didn't have to consult or defer to anyone except, occasionally, my determined little six-year-old! Emmie and I developed a special bond on the road, and as we settled into our travel groove we operated as a team. We not only shared every day together, we shared every step along the way – the decisions, the adventures, the challenges and the many amazing highs. Travelling with Emmie showed me I could achieve so much more than I ever thought possible and built me into a confident, more self-aware person. If you're travelling as a solo parent the challenges may be a little more daunting and sometimes you may wish for an extra set of hands, but the bonds you forge with your children as you explore, learn and adventure together will be some of the sweetest and most enduring of your lives.
Evie Farrell, Mumpack Travel

Multigenerational trips

If your children are lucky enough to have grandparents around with the time and inclination to come on holiday with you, then it's definitely worth considering asking them to join you. Taking a trip with grandparents and children is not a small undertaking, but it can be an incredibly rewarding holiday, with three generations getting a chance to bond, hopefully at least a small amount of babysitting or shared childcare and potentially even a financial contribution. Sow the seed gently before you actually ask the question. While many grandparents will jump at the chance, some may not want to join you but may feel duty bound to accept, which is not a great starting point. Older family friends can also be good travelling companions if they enjoy spending time with your kids.

Before you book, sit down and have a talk with everyone about their expectations for the trip: a good idea is to ask everyone to name one thing that they really want to do so you can be sure you're not leaving anyone out. Then think about the logistics. Is getting six, seven or more people of all different ages through a busy airport going to be really quite hard work for all concerned? Would it be better to drive or fly separately? Is there enough to do that will keep all the generations busy, factoring in possibly different energy levels? Do you have a wet weather plan? Is a rental house the best option in terms of keeping costs down but giving everyone space, or would your larger family prefer a hotel? Who is paying and for what? Even the most generous of grandparents don't want to feel taken advantage of, so having a straightforward chat about finances before you go is a good idea. If you are going to want them to look after the kids a bit while you do something, ask if this would be possible before you go. And do as you would have your children do: be polite and thank them for any help they give you.

Try to avoid making assumptions about what the grandparents might do (especially around anticipated pet peeves). But do recognise the knowledge and expertise the older generation can bring to your planning and your trip. They are an important part of your

© ALISTAIR BERG / GETTY IMAGES

Travelling with another family can be a really positive experience as the kids get ready-made playmates while the adults get to share the planning, logistics and childcare while spending time with their friends. However, before you take the plunge check that your travel styles are pretty similar – if you like to carefully plan everything then going away with a more spontaneous family could cause stress on your trip (alternatively, you could embrace the change). Likewise if your family takes ages to get going in the morning but your friends like to set off at the crack of dawn, you may find being away for a week together isn't a good fit. And it's not just the adults that need to cooperate. Negotiating endless squabbles is no fun for anyone and a surefire way to test even the strongest of parent friendships. Start with a short trip or stay in quarters that give everyone breathing room as a first trial run.

holiday team and their skills and ideas need to be considered and listened to. Talk to each other about what you are bringing, as this is a good opportunity to share the packing, and avoid bringing multiples of basics.

Lastly remember quality over quantity. Even the closest of families start to struggle with too long in each other's company. Keep it short and sweet to leave everyone hungry for more. Overexposure can lead to frazzled nerves, especially on a frenetic itinerary. Planned space apart for separate activities during the trip can help as well.

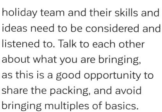

Get the kids involved

INVOLVE YOUR CHILDREN IN THE BUDGET FOR THE TRIP

TALK THROUGH THE PROPOSED PLANS FOR EACH DAY THE NIGHT BEFORE WITH THE KIDS

BE REALLY BRAVE AND LET THE CHILDREN PLAN A DAY EACH

It's really important that they learn about handling money and how to weigh up different expenditures. Encourage them to save their own money if they want spending money to use as they like for the trip.

Use each day to talk with the kids about what the next day's plans are, and what they are interested in doing. An open discussion means everyone feels involved and has a chance to voice what they want to do.

Be really, really brave by turning over the reins to your kids and even let them make some mistakes. After all it's through mistakes that we learn.

LET THEM CHOOSE WHAT'S FOR DINNER

GET THE KIDS TO BE THE TOUR LEADERS FOR A PARTICULAR SITE

TAKE A SKETCH PAD AND PENCILS

Give each child a day when they decide what you have for dinner or where you go for lunch, and avoid endless trips to McDonald's with the caveat that it has to have some link to the local cuisine.

They can read up before you go, write some notes about what they want to show you and discuss. You'll be surprised at what you can learn from them.

Even the most reluctant young artist can use what they are looking at for inspiration, and it's a lovely souvenir to take home. Plus, it helps fend off boredom during wait times.

FIND BOOKS THAT ARE SET IN OR LINKED TO PLACES YOU ARE VISITING

Fiction can be an imaginative way of bringing a place to life, and well-illustrated nonfiction reference books are incredible resources for teaching kids about where they are visiting.

TEACH EVERYONE SOME BASIC WORDS IN THE LANGUAGE OF THE COUNTRY YOU ARE IN

Not only is this polite but it opens so many doors when someone hears a child say please or thank you in their language.

BRING YOUR OWN INTERACTIVE FUN

Take a tennis ball or small inflatable football along to play with, as this can serve (no pun intended) as a way to get your kids interacting with local or other visiting children.

Left: Glenfinnan Railway Viaduct in Scotland with the Jacobite steam train. Above: Sketching while on holiday.

FAMILY TRAVEL HANDBOOK

Escape to the great outdoors

Most parents quickly learn that getting their children out of the home and into the fresh air improves everyone's mood. It's the change of scene, the literal broadening of horizons by seeing more of the sky and the chance to expend pent-up energy. Move that change of scene into the natural world and you take the experience to a different level: as adults we know that being in nature is good for our souls, and it's no different for little people. Cartwheeling around a field, climbing a tree, riding a bike along an old bridle path or farm track, scaling some rocks, paddling in the sea, kayaking round an inlet – all these things and many more keep children active, build their self-esteem, teach them about taking risks and show them how important it is to preserve our natural world.

Wherever you live, but especially if you are based in a city, travelling with your children provides a good opportunity to spend more time in the countryside or wilderness. Some of the best outdoor pleasures are the simplest: go for a local walk at different times of the day and ask your children to talk about what they can see and hear and feel. A good first trip with tiny babies can be to get

© CHRIS BEAVON / GETTY IMAGES

Opposite: A campfire and Cathedral Lake, Yosemite. Left: The lavender fields in Provence.

away in the car to somewhere you can walk with them in a sling (although making sure they don't get too hot or too cold can limit how far you can go). With toddlers, consider staying on a working farm or basing yourself in a rental somewhere in the countryside with a petting zoo or farm to visit, restored trains to take chugging through the countryside or living museums to potter around. These all can provide a good pace with plenty of fresh-air activities for the morning and a place to return to for naptime (and much-needed down time for parents). As children get older it's a joy to start to do more challenging physical activities with them, and the rewarding sense of achievement strengthens the family bond. For teenagers,

activities can be an important way to reconnect with each other. Finding something you all enjoy doing together takes the emphasis off the family unit (which can be stifling for teens) and gives you a new focus. Often this can be a chance for teens to get some independence too, either through signing up for a group-based activity with people their age or through giving them more responsibility such as reading maps and leading the way on a hike.

If there's something you've always enjoyed doing such as hiking, sailing or skiing, the chances are high that you will want to introduce your kids to it. Be prepared to take things slowly, learn from successes and from mistakes and keep the ultimate goal in sight. It's hard to

be active with little people, but by establishing early on that your family likes to get out in nature whenever possible, you reap the rewards as the children get older, can do more by themselves and actively choose to spend their trips being out and about in the fresh air. Fellow enthusiasts who are parents of older kids can be excellent sources of ideas if your little ones are struggling.

National parks or protected areas of natural beauty are a good place to start in any destination you visit. In some places the organisations looking after these areas have excellent programmes designed to get children engaged and involved. Try the Junior Ranger initiative in the US, the UK's imaginative Forestry Commission and WilderQuest in Australia.

FAMILY TRAVEL HANDBOOK

Camping

Whether you love or loathe camping, it's hard to deny that it's a very cost-effective way to travel as a family and that most kids absolutely adore the freedom, fresh air and excitement that comes from living temporarily under canvas. You can take even the youngest family members on a camping trip, living at their pace with early nights (except at big campsites where there might be evening entertainment) and getting up as the sun rises.

If you're not totally convinced, borrow whatever camping gear you're missing and start by giving it a go for a couple of nights to see if it works for your family. If you are really not sure, a good place to begin is with an organisation such as Eurocamp in Europe, where the tent is set up for you, you sleep on camp beds rather than the ground and kitchen equipment is provided. Choose a site with the children's age and the type of holiday you are after in mind. Teenagers might be bored senseless by a small site in the wilds, but a busy campsite near a beach might not suit a family with toddlers. Be aware that the nicest sites book up quickly, especially during school holidays. Another option is to rent a cabin to get close to nature without being entirely exposed to it.

Camping enthusiasts are a friendly fraternity and there are many sites dedicated to sharing knowledge on kit and gear, sites, packing lists and so on. Lean on their expertise, but remember that you'll probably forget something essential, and that's OK. Like most things in life, the first time you do it will be a big learning curve – many a marriage or partnership has wavered during the erection of a large family tent – but you'll soon get an idea of whether you like it enough to do it again. For many, campfires and s'mores are a classic childhood memory that parents and kids alike adore.

Make sure you get the kids involved – older children can help with the tent, younger

© JOHNER IMAGES / GETTY IMAGES

© OLIVEROMG / SHUTTERSTOCK

Opposite: Van camping in Norway. Above: Lake camping and s'mores. Below: A kayaking adventure.

children can pump mattresses, and working together to prepare your meals is good teamwork. And then there's the washing up. You'll be amazed how the most boring chores suddenly become an object of enthusiasm when you're in the woods.

If sleeping under canvas or in a cabin isn't quite your thing, it's worth exploring renting (or even buying) a campervan or RV (short for 'residential vehicle'). Many families swear by the ease of having everything in one place, the flexibility and freedom it brings and the ability to enjoy the romance of the open road as a family. If you're doing a big road trip or taking a year (or longer) to travel with your kids, an RV can be an excellent and cost-effective option. If nothing else, by the end of it you can be sure you will all know each other very, very well.

Hiking

Hiking with children can bestow them with a love of the outdoors and a thirst for exploration that lasts a lifetime, but it's not something you can deliver overnight. The key is to start small with shorter strolls and build to bigger missions. Tailor treks to suit the capabilities of the youngest or least outdoorsy member of your group. Sticking to routes that are comfortably below 10km (or 6 miles) until kids are 10 years old (or under 2km, just over a mile, for the under fives) is a good rule of thumb. You can make it fun by finding trails that provide a sense of achievement, a historical story to learn, animals to watch out for or tree-dwelling fairies to catch. Most kids love exploring rock pools, caves and dunes, so coastal walks are always a hit.

Get the children involved in the planning to really engage their interest, let them route-find (with help if required) and then make sure you review

Clockwise from top: Mother and daughter at Thurston Lava Tube, Hawaii; Mt Mitchell State Park; exploring the Tyrol; hiking Lake Bled, Slovenia.

the route at the end. Walking with other children can work wonders in helping the miles pass, but beware signs of mutiny – whining is highly contagious and will quickly spread through a gaggle of kids. Keep everyone enthusiastic by rewarding positive attitudes and achievements. And use an arsenal of games such as I Spy, 20 Questions and the Alphabet Game (where you have to name things such as animals, cities or people you know for each letter of the alphabet) up your sleeve.

Make sure you pack plenty of warm and waterproof clothing (layers are always best), and take lots of food to keep the kids fuelled. Healthy snacks such as fruit and nuts are ideal, and remember, a sweet treat delivered at the right moment – at the summit of a big climb, for example – can perform magic tricks for morale.

Encourage children to prepare their own small backpack with a mixture of essential equipment and fun extras: a magnifying glass for inspecting insects; a torch/flashlight for caves, hollow trees and emergencies; binoculars for wildlife spotting; and a camera to catch shots of the grown-ups falling over.

Once kids are comfortable with tackling trails, you can increase the adventure level and keep them excited by doing an overnight hike. Most youngsters find the concept of sleeping outside absolutely captivating, and it's still possible to keep things comfortable in the backcountry with hot chocolate and toasted marshmallows, while stargazing in the wilderness is truly mind-blowing for young and old. If you're wild camping, do make sure it's legal. In England, Dartmoor has legal wild camping, while in Yellowstone National Park you can even hire a llama to tote your bags.

FAMILY TRAVEL HANDBOOK

Get aquatic

Tempted by the idea of a family boat trip? Do you love kayaking or have you always wanted to go fly-fishing? There are plenty of possibilities for enjoying water with your kids; it all depends on the age of your kids, your preferences and – of course – some planning. Start with basic swimming lessons, and soon the horizon will be your limit.

For families that love to swim there's no better place than a beach or water park in the sunshine. But if you are ready for something different, don't forget the joy of watching the world underwater. Grabbing a snorkel and mask for each child is a lovely way to introduce them to the aquatic world.

Go a step further and after the age of eight (or 12 according to some experts) you can introduce them to scuba diving. Your child must want to dive, be a competent swimmer and be able to take instruction and make sound judgements. Research the best destinations for beginners, find dive centres that cater specifically for children (and if you are English-speaking, instruct in English) and check what are the right affiliations for the centres to have (dive instructors are typically either PADI or SSI certified). Contacts may be necessary for anyone with prescription lenses.

Paddling around a calm body of water in a kayak or canoe can be great fun, but especially if you aren't an experienced paddler yourself you need to take precautions. Make sure you have one adult to one child, and ensure everyone can swim (and that you know how strong their swimming is) and understands the wet-exit procedure. Start with smaller outings to begin with. As a general rule of thumb, children under eight aren't ready to paddle the bow of either a kayak or canoe. Even wilder is tubing or whitewater rafting, both with more adrenaline rushes but requiring strong safety protocols. For adventure at sea, kite-sailing, surfing and paddleboarding are all exciting physical challenges suitable for older children.

If you are looking for a bigger boat experience, taking a canal barge trip in Europe can be great fun. Although quite pricey, after a short lesson in dealing with the boat you are the skipper and the kids will love getting involved in navigating the locks. If you're based somewhere

Above: Surf school in Santa Theresa, Costa Rica. Left: Snorkelling a reef.

The fun you can have as a family at the beach is well known, but feeling the sand between your toes in the desert can be an unforgettable experience as well. Climb the dunes, try sand boarding, take a camel ride or learn about desert life with a local guide. Depending on where you are in the world and how old your kids are, you can also take a hot-air balloon, go hiking or try a quad bike. The otherwordly landscape you often find when visiting deserts tends to captivate children's imaginations, and the whole family will benefit from their improved understanding of desert cultures. But camping can take the whole experience to another level. Not only do you get to see the most incredible night skies but it's a proper adventure to camp in the desert. Who needs sleep when you can see the desert come to life and do some serious stargazing?

with an extensive canal system like the UK, France or the Netherlands, then a day trip to practice can be a good chance to see if your family are going to enjoy this type of trip. In terms of sailing boats, you can take a child sailing from an early age – especially if you sail with a crew. It's common sense that the most difficult age is when a child is learning to walk (you cannot take your eyes off a toddler when you are on board) and you must never leave a child under six alone on a boat. For a first expedition by boat, it's best to go for a short trip: discover Luxor and Karnak on board a traditional felucca, island-hop in Greece or take a Turkish gulet and enjoy the tranquility of the beautiful coves.

Check in advance that there are life jackets to fit your children and that they understand the safety requirements. Asking them to repeat back to you what they've learnt is a good test. It's always colder out at sea so take layers and also sun protection. Don't forget motion sickness tablets (children need their own versions), ginger biscuits to help with mild nausea and the trick of looking at the horizon and getting plenty of fresh air. Kids will love the novelty.

FAMILY TRAVEL HANDBOOK

Winter activities

The easiest way to get your kids out enjoying the snow is to get them dressed warmly and head to the nearest hill after a snowfall. Seeing their local world transformed by the white stuff is a pretty magical experience, and most kids love hurtling at high speeds on a bit of plastic.

However, if you are lucky enough to live near ski resorts or have the funds to take the whole family away, then nothing beats skiing or snowboarding. If you can already ski yourself, then chances are you want to introduce your kids to it; if you're new to skiing, then learning the sport together can be a fantastic experience – as long as you are prepared for the fact your kids will quickly be better than you are! Skiing can be scary, so learning to ski teaches kids to face their fears and have confidence; by being scared we learn how to be brave. It also teaches children that practice makes progress, the importance of communicating (where are we all going to meet, how do you know this run is appropriate, and

so on) and also how important it is to be aware of other people, judge risks and be physically fit.

If your family is already pretty good at hiking you can try snow treks, but remember it's harder work to walk on snow than dry land, so be realistic with what you attempt. Snowshoes or cross-country skis will add some variety (and a fun new skill to master).

The key for enjoying outdoor activities in the snow with kids is to make sure they've got the right clothing and then keep them moving so they stay warm. Waterproof warm trousers, coats and gloves, base layers (top and bottom) that are made of wool, good socks that fit properly and a snood that can double as a balaclava under a hat or helmet are essential.

© AMBRE HALLER / GETTY IMAGES

Clockwise from top: Downhill skiing, Bavaria; kicksledding in Tromsø; Val d'Isère in the Alps; tobogganing in Alberta, Canada.

Travelling sustainably with kids

Interacting with nature comes with an important responsibility: we have to show our children how to look after our natural world and how to minimise our impact.

1

Talk to your kids about the cleanest ways to get around for the environment; if you like to travel, chances are you will take planes from time to time, but you can discuss with your children a plan for minimising the trips you take by plane – and also by car. Teach them the importance of relying on trains, bikes and public transport.

 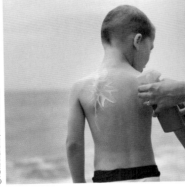

Left to right: juvenile hawksbill sea turtle; applying sun protection; cross-country skiing.

2

Consider eco-friendly accommodation options and environmentally-friendly ways to get around, and work out how you can get off the beaten track and help spread out the impact of tourists in a destination.

3

Choose a responsible tour operator who can help you make the right decisions.

4

Take reusable water bottles, bags, crockery and cutlery and use them whenever you can. Don't stop recycling just because you are not at home. Say no to plastic straws unless they're needed for health. reasons.

5

The message to protect your children from sun exposure is important, but be aware too of the impact of the chemicals in sun cream on aquatic life and use oxybenzone-free formulas like mineral options. Some places have banned non-environmentally friendly compounds, so check before you go.

© SCOTT CRAMER / GETTY IMAGES

6

Teach your kids the importance of leaving no trace: when out in nature you need to stay on the trails, follow park rules, leave everything as you find it and take litter home.

7

Support local enterprises where possible. Shop locally at markets rather than larger supermarkets; it's more fun for the kids to explore, a great way to learn about a region and you can make the most of your reusable bags.

8

Some activities (such as skiing) will require new purchases, but think twice before buying lots of new things. Can you borrow the gear instead?

9

Animal interactions can be harmful for all involved, so consider carefully here. Watching wildlife from afar is fine, but be wary of swimming with sea creatures or riding an elephant.

10

Some parks run volunteer programmes where families can help build trails. Can you combine your holiday with giving back? Sea turtle conservation is a perennial favourite.

Get the kids involved

★

Getting kids involved at the very start of planning a trip creates a successful family adventure in the outdoors and gives them a strong connection to nature.

★

Have the kids talk through their opinion on the ethics of zoos and wildlife-viewing vs interactive experiences. They can also help you pick a carbon offset charity for donations.

★

If you have a GPS unit, add an extra layer of interest to a nature walk with a spot of geocaching.

★

Let your children set the pace. They may want to climb trees, play hide-and-seek, skim stones, kick autumn leaves around, collect pebbles and pick blackberries along the way, and so they should – it's all part of the outdoor experience.

What are you waiting for?

If the idea of taking your children away travelling is still feeling like a pretty big challenge, it can help to reframe it in your mind as an adventure. After all, adventures are exciting, and thinking of your next trip as one can remind you that pushing your collective comfort zone will strengthen your bonds, create those all-important memories and help all of you grow as individuals.

When balancing family, work and other commitments, it's completely natural that we gravitate to our comfort zone. Having a routine and dealing with what is familiar to us means we can know what to expect next. Stress isn't a nice feeling and most of us are hardwired to minimise it where possible.

However, learning how to push yourself out of that comfort zone is a key skill we need to teach our children. By taking on a challenge, we open ourselves up to things going right and also to things going wrong. We learn best when we make mistakes, but you need to take a risk to make a mistake. When we take a risk and it goes right, we enjoy a sense of accomplishment and satisfaction that we did something good. Accepting mistakes, growing as a result of them, feeling positive when you make the right call: this process boosts self-esteem, encourages creativity and makes life interesting.

Kids are constantly stepping out of their comfort zone as they learn life skills, from their first steps to taking swimming lessons and navigating a classroom. They need the security of routine at home, but here's where travel really comes into its own: when you travel with your kids you have a unique opportunity to role model for them how to assess the risk and take it, deal with things that go wrong and revel in it when they go right.

For many of us, exploring the world starts on our own doorstep, and this is a brilliant place to begin to push our own boundaries. In this chapter we have ideas for getting started exploring within your local area and then, when you are ready, suggestions for how to introduce a more adventurous element to your family trips. Perhaps the biggest adventure you can have with your kids is to decide to travel permanently, so this chapter finishes with advice on how to prepare for that big trip.

Left: On safari in Etosha National Park, Namibia.
Below: Sunset on Sanibel Island's beach, Florida.

Start small

Getting out and about exploring what's nearby, your local region or even different parts of your own country, are all solid ways to build your confidence as a travelling parent.

BE A BACKYARD EXPLORER

Most of us are already pretty familiar with where we live, but you can turn a simple trip to your local park or shops into something much more imaginative, thereby creating a love of exploring and the ability to look at familiar things in a new way. These activities get your kids engaging with their home environment.

★
Start by drawing your street from memory. Alternatively, be a cartographer for a day and create your own local map.

★
Create a list of ten things you might see when out and about and challenge a friend to spot them all.

★
Use the alphabet and name something in your area for each letter.

★
Spend 15 minutes sitting still quietly somewhere relatively hidden and record all the birds, insects and animals you see.

★
Turn this into a number challenge. Start with finding a number '1' and go around the neighbourhood collecting numbers in order.

★
Find five local street names and investigate their meaning.

★
Keep a weather chart: you can make rain gauges and wind vanes and then record what they tell you, or simply just note what the weather is and how it makes you feel.

★
Lie on the ground and draw what you see: it might be the tops of a tree, a funny-shaped cloud or a crisscross of flight paths.

© EDUCATION IMAGES / GETTY IMAGES

© FABRICE LEROUGE / GETTY IMAGES

Try a staycation

A staycation can mean different things to different people, but here we're talking about taking a holiday from work and making the most of what's available to you from home. This obviously saves on transport and accommodation costs, but it does require parents fully shutting off work and chores to be in vacation mode while at home – no staying plugged in! These activities recharge everyone's curiosity.

VISIT SOMEWHERE YOU'VE NEVER BEEN BEFORE BY PUBLIC TRANSPORT

You never know what hidden gems you will unearth in your own neighbourhood until you go looking. Just visiting somewhere new can bring a whole new perspective for a day. Travelling by public transport adds another dimension, as you can teach the kids about reading timetables, waiting patiently and how to behave in shared public space such as a train, bus or tram.

LET THE KIDS TAKE CHARGE

It's refreshing (if not a little challenging) to let go of plans for a day out and let the kids make them. Of course you have to set parameters around cost, food and logistics, but set these out clearly at the start and then see where your children take you. It can be an informative and fascinating way to get to know a different side of your local area and you can guarantee that the kids will love it and talk about it for a long time afterwards.

CHANGE THE SLEEPING ARRANGEMENTS

Have a sleepover all in one room, make a cosy den out of cushions and blankets or even set up camp in your garden. Sleeping under canvas is huge fun for kids and you can make hot chocolate and do some stargazing or set up a projector and sheet to watch an outdoor movie. Or, whether you are inside or outside, just light some candles, put on a vacation soundtrack and play some board games.

BE SPONTANEOUS

So much of life with kids is regulated around school and weekend activities. Use a staycation to be properly spontaneous and see what you do by the end of your days together. Check for last-minute discounts at your local theatres, see what's on at your local museum and find a new place to take a fancy picnic, or go on a challenging hike or bike ride.

SET A DAILY CHALLENGE

Set yourselves a challenge to find or try one new thing for every day of your staycation. This could be picking fruit or vegetables at a local farm, cooking a particular dish together, helping out as volunteers somewhere or all trying to read a book in a day (hold a 'book club' to discuss it after). Anything that pushes that collective comfort zone!

Go domestic

When you are done exploring your backyard and you've survived the holiday at home, it's time to up the ante and find yourselves a little getaway elsewhere within your home country. In doing so, you learn about how it works to transplant your family to a new place within the safety net of the same language, culture and money. A road trip to some of the old haunts you loved to visit as a child or even just to see a relative or friend is a great place to start. It's all about building your confidence. Each time you take your kids on a new and different travel experience you learn something which encourages you to try it again. The following ideas can get you started.

★
Follow a friend's recommendation and book accommodations they've already tried and tested.

★
Indulge your child's passion for trains, science, cooking, drawing or whatever else is their current interest by finding a fun way to get involved.

★
Find a theme park you know your kids will love and splurge with a hotel on site.

★
Hire a villa or condo by the beach and switch off for a few days.

© ANTON_IVANOV / SHUTTERSTOCK

Volunteer together

If you want to give back to the communities your family visits, make a genuine connection with local people, meet like-minded travellers and build everyone's skills, then volunteering when you are away can be an incredible experience for your family. Above all else it teaches your kids how important it is to help others. And it definitely pushes everyone out of their comfort zone. However, volunteering has to be done properly if you don't want to leave a damaging legacy behind you; the below tips are good to keep in mind.

★ Do your homework before you go so you are comfortable that your family is going to be making a long-term positive contribution. A great resource is the dedicated family volunteer programme through www.volunteerhq.org.

★ Choose the right organisation. Read all about what they do and make sure it aligns with your family's values.

★ Check that the organisation is legitimate: they should be registered in the country and with their local government and should require certain checks on you before you can turn up.

★ Contact the organisation before you go to make sure they need your help. This is especially important for families, as accommodating larger groups of varying ages can be more complicated.

★ Ask them what help they need, rather than telling them what you can all do.

★ Check that volunteering is really the best use of your time, as opposed to – for example – fundraising as a family at home. Remember too that volunteering for just a short period of time may be great for your family but it can be disruptive to the organisation that you want to help.

★ Always think: if my family were in need of assistance, would my family's services be helpful?

★ If you are comfortable that you have found the right organisation, still ask questions about how they work with volunteer families to be sure the experience is going to work for them and you. Where are you all going to stay while you are volunteering and how are you going to find time to spend together as a family?

★ Once you're happy you've found the right opportunity to help, you need to prepare your kids as much as you can before you arrive, showing them photographs and explaining what you are going to be doing.

★ When you are there it's all about being a role model to your kids: work hard, get involved, be respectful. Show your kids how to be a good volunteer and you set them up for life with a healthy and respectful attitude to giving back.

87

Push your collective comfort zone

As you take more trips with your kids and learn about what works for you and your family, at some point you may feel ready to push yourselves to the next level, especially as children get older and are able to handle more physical challenges and take instruction better. A good place to start might be to do something adventurous for a day trip within your 'normal' holiday. For example, you may enjoy exploring national parks from a hotel or condo base, but what about arranging to camp for one night? Can you rent bikes and spend a day exploring on two wheels? Is there a river to kayak down, a peak to hike up or a rock to scale? If you are on a city break, what about getting involved in something you don't normally do, such as an art workshop, cooking course or language lesson?

It's important to remember that being adventurous can be cultural as well as physical. Taking your family to a destination with a culture very different to your own is an adventure in itself as you all learn to navigate different social

Above: A cooking class can be great fun for all involved.

cues, different food, different languages, different ways of dressing and so on. You can be more adventurous with your destination choice while sticking to activities you know you are all comfortable with when you are there. Taking a long-haul flight for the first time with kids in tow can be enough of an adventure! Equally, taking a city break, especially to a large frenetic city such as New York, London or Paris, is an adventure even if culturally it's familiar and you're not necessarily

pushing yourselves with physical challenges. For many families, jumping on the tube or metro gets the heart rate soaring, while working out the best way to explore world-famous sites along with everyone else is a challenge in itself.

Prepare children for culture shock

The more adventurous your destination the higher the likelihood that you are going to encounter a culture very different to their own. Here's how to lay some good groundwork before you go:

★ Find books, videos, films and music set in your destination and enjoy them together.

★ Let everyone in the family know it's normal to feel a bit out of sorts in a new and unfamiliar destination. Encourage kids to talk about how they are feeling and make sure you spend time properly listening as well as answering.

© WESTEND61 / GETTY IMAGES

Above: On Thailand's Khao San Road. Below left: The coast of Dubrovnik.

★ With food, talk about what they can expect to eat, what they might like and what they might like to try. Remind them how important it is to be respectful of other people's choices – they may not like the food they are offered, but it may be the local delicacy and an honour to be served it. Politeness is key!

★ Once you arrive, try to stick to a routine if you can, as small children take comfort in the familiar. Build some downtime into your days for everyone to breathe out, and bring a couple of familiar things from home (including snacks) to help with the adjustment process.

★ Read up yourself on the culture of the destination and talk to your kids about what to expect. Remind your kids that generalisations don't always apply, but it does help to discuss expectations of behaviour as well as the importance of being polite and remembering that not everyone has the same habits they do.

Adventure destinations

If you've had a few days here and there trying more adventurous activities as part of your holidays and your kids are old enough for you all to feel ready to do a trip where you push yourselves, the following destinations offer a good mix of adrenaline-pumping options with a family-friendly infrastructure.

ICELAND

Within one trip, your family can go dogsledding, whale watching and glacier trekking, as well as see the Northern Lights, descend into the crater of an active volcano and spend plenty of time jumping in and out of thermal pools.

MARRAKESH, MOROCCO

The call to prayer; snake charmers plying their trade; tiny alleys to explore; shops with wares piled high; spices, tagines and fresh juices to sample – a visit to the medina in Marrakesh is an adventure for the senses.

SOUTH AFRICA

Seeing animals in the wild scores pretty high on the adventure meter for most people, and Kruger National Park works well for families due to the high likelihood of spotting animals, the family-friendly lodges and the relatively small distances involved.

NEW ZEALAND

Its natural beauty and excellent reputation for outdoor pursuits make the country a popular destination for families. Hiring a camper-van gives you the freedom of the open road and the fun of outdoor life without having to camp each night.

SNOWDONIA, UK

Bounce on trampolines hidden within caves, fly through the air on a giant swing and surf an inland lagoon. Kids will also love adventuring through history at the many castles, climbing to the top of Snowdon and resting weary legs on a narrow-gauge railway.

WASHINGTON, DC, USA

Exploring a world-famous city is an adventure in itself. In DC you can combine learning the art of espionage at the International Spy Museum with a dose of history from the many excellent child-friendly museums. Take the elevator ride to the top of the Washington Monument and enjoy paddle boating in the Tidal Basin.

JAPAN

For much of the world a visit to Japan is a cultural adventure. It's also a dream come true for your robot-loving, game-playing, tech-happy teen, making it a good destination for families balancing different demands.

SOUTHWESTERN AUSTRALIA

From a 600m-long treetop walk in the Valley of the Giants to exploring caves in the Margaret River region, to whale watching, beachcombing, riding bikes and climbing trees, there is no shortage of fun and exciting activities to try here.

SRI LANKA

Between elephants and trains, ancient temples and beaches, forts and natural parks, there's so much to explore and the warm welcome for families is something to treasure. Check current security updates, but don't entirely rule out this gem.

MALAYSIA

If you're looking to dip your family's toes into Southeast Asia, Malaysia is a great place to start. The mix of cultures allows just enough of the familiar (colonial architecture, shopping centres, Western food) for when the exotic (the heat, the flavours, the crowds) becomes overwhelming.

Three top tips for developing your family's sense of adventure

Your family's sense of adventure is like a muscle; if you exercise it regularly you'll be surprised how quickly it develops. Start by working it in small ways, going on manageable adventures from your own doorstep. When our kids were little we occasionally paddled to the supermarket in a canoe!

Soon you'll be fit enough to pack a day sack for a bigger adventure. This needn't necessarily involve a hike up Helvellyn or a scramble up Scafell Pike. You might want to try some gentle fell running or orienteering as a family on a local hill. You could take a wild swim in a lake or go mountain biking on a forest trail. You could download a Treasure Trail and follow it around your local town or take everyone on a bug hunt in the woods.

Once you have got the hang of 9–5 adventures, I recommend you grab a sleeping bag and try the 5–9 variety by sleeping out under the stars. Take a tent to protect your kit and kids from rain or early morning dew, or make your own shelter with a tarp or branches. Don't forget to pack supplies for a sunrise breakfast. Exercising those adventure muscles can make a family very hungry.

Kirstie Pelling, Family Adventure Project

Become a world nomad

Perhaps the ultimate move in stepping out of your comfort zone is to quit work, rent out the family home and take off to explore the world on an extended journey. It's a step that plenty of parents would love to take, but the thought of planning such a mammoth trip can be daunting – especially when it takes all your energy just to get the kids out the door. However, it is easier than you might think.

MAKE THE DECISION AND STICK TO IT

There are positives and negatives to a round-the-world trip with kids at any age. Travelling with babies or toddlers is cheaper but, while the whole experience will stay with them for life, it's unlikely that they will remember many of the details about the trip. Older children will form longer-lasting memories, but you'll need to think more about their education. Teenagers can handle more intrepid undertakings, but close friendships and looming exams may mean they'll take more convincing. Worry too much about the 'right' time to go and you might never take the plunge. Just choose a date and get planning. You won't regret it.

© SAMOT / SHUTTERSTOCK

ARRANGE TIME APART

For everyone's sanity, take turns with one parent watching the kids while the other gets some alone time, hire a babysitter and have a grown-up night out, or treat yourself to a stay in a hotel with a kids club. Allowing your kids a break from each other can also save everyone some headaches. If you're travelling with a partner, divide and conquer by each of you taking a child or two off from the others for a day.

© DRAZEN_ / GETTY IMAGES

BUDGET, BUDGET, BUDGET

Running out of cash halfway across the world is best avoided, so it can help to work out a maximum weekly budget and stick to it – with money put aside for emergencies and occasional splurges. You'll need to adjust the budget depending on where you are in the world though. If you're on a tight budget, spend the bulk of your time in cheaper countries. You'll blow through money faster in North America and Western Europe than you would in Thailand, Sri Lanka or India for example.

To save cash, try camping or staying in hostels (many of which are family-friendly these days), and cooking your own food rather than eating out for every meal. Couchsurfing (www.couchsurfing.com) or housesitting will save you money while allowing your family to experience life as the locals live it. Some families even plan their long-term travel around the FIRE (financial independence, retire early) movement, setting up a stash of investments by careful saving and then retiring early to take on the nomad life.

© PHILIP LEE HARVEY / LONELY PLANET

CHOOSE YOUR OWN TRAVEL STYLE

While travelling with babies and toddlers needn't preclude adventurous travel, some destinations – Southeast Asia, for example – are more tot-friendly than others. With older children and teenagers you could explore more challenging options such as a camping safari in the African bush or even hiking in the Himalayas.

Don't forget: a round-the-world adventure needn't involve a multi-stop plane ticket and a backpack; travelling overland in a camper-van is a fun and flexible way to travel, or you could even try cycling across a continent or navigating the oceans in a sailboat.

FAMILY TRAVEL HANDBOOK

PACK LIGHT AND SMART

Pack as little as possible, whether you are lugging around baby paraphernalia or travelling with older kids who can carry their own stuff. You can buy nappies/diapers, baby food and even clothes as you go along – and you may well need to anyway, given the rate at which most children grow.

Must-haves include a comfort object or two for small children, a lightweight sling for babies and toddlers, and a tablet or laptop loaded with games and movies for when the inevitable cries of boredom strike. A small backpack that young children can pack and carry themselves is a great way of involving them in the preparations.

GET THE KIDS INVOLVED

Letting the kids take part in the day-to-day decision-making is all part of the fun. Ask them for their ideas of what to do and where to visit; encourage them to write or draw in a journal daily; or give them their own child-friendly camera to capture the world from their own perspective.

You may need to move slower than you did in your pre-children days. Most kids won't take kindly to rushing around ticking off high-profile sites; it's more relaxing for all involved to spend several days, weeks, or even months in each destination.

Right: Opportunities for exploration abound on the road, but may take some planning.

©HERO IMAGES / GETTY IMAGES

© JUSTIN PAGET / GETTY IMAGES

MAKE A PLAN FOR EDUCATION

If you're travelling for any serious length of time with children of school age, you need to think about and agree as a family how you want to approach education. Some families 'unschool', others 'world school' and yet more may 'home educate while on the road'. There's no right or wrong option but it pays to do your research.

STAY HEALTHY ON THE ROAD

Looking after your family's health is, of course, a top priority. Before you go, arrange the requisite vaccinations and anti-malarials in plenty of time, and remember that some jabs (typhoid for one) can't be given before a certain age. Carry a good first aid kit and discuss in advance what to do in an emergency; comprehensive travel insurance is a must.

While it pays to be prepared, with all the fresh air and exercise you'll likely be getting on the road, plus new, varied foods and plenty of mood-boosting family time, chances are you'll all be healthier than ever while you're away.

We've found, over the last five years on the road, that taking our boys to the source has been a superb way for them to learn about the world. Why be stuck with a book and a classroom? They can be out there, seeing, touching and experiencing history, cultures, geography and every incredible thing the world has to offer.

We love that if the boys want to learn more about a favourite topic, we can take them to the best place to deepen their knowledge, be that the pyramids, Tikal, The Ganges, the Dalí Museum, Mount Everest or a peasant village in Romania. They have their freedom, they're meeting diverse people of all ages and backgrounds and they're loving their lives. As an added bonus we parents get to spend their entire childhoods with them, not just school holidays.
Alyson Long,
World Travel Family

Let your kids roam free

We couldn't have a chapter on being adventurous without covering one of the biggest challenges facing parents who love to travel. If you've successfully shown your kids how amazing it is to travel the world, then there will come a day when they will set foot on a trip without you there to guide them. This really is an adventure for both you and them. Will they remember all the invaluable lessons that you have taught them during your many trips as a family? Will you handle the anxiety of not knowing how they are dealing with different situations? Watching your grown or growing child set off on an independent trip is daunting, but there are many reasons why it's absolutely necessary to support and encourage them doing so. Travelling will teach them amazing lessons.

LEARN TO SOLVE PROBLEMS

If they don't already know how to solve problems by themselves, they will by the time they get back. From simple tasks such as booking train or plane tickets and finding a place to stay, to working out what to do after missing a train and when bank cards are swallowed or luggage is lost, every problem solved is a step in the right direction. Facing these situations increases adaptability and self-assurance.

GAIN NEW PERSPECTIVES

With travel often comes a greater level of compassion, through increased exposure to lifestyles and circumstances that differ from our own – invaluable lessons at any stage in life, but especially for a young adult. Travel can also overturn stereotypes and reveal a fresh view of the world.

UNLOCK NEW LANGUAGE SKILLS

Travelling often presents the chance to pick up another language; immersive learning is often the fastest route. The desire to properly pursue a language can emerge from time spent overseas, holding great benefits for when a child returns home and elevating their employment prospects as well as providing a deeper connection to people met while abroad.

© KLAUS VEDFELT / GETTY IMAGES

AND FINALLY...

If you're struggling with the idea of your baby flinging himself off a bungee bridge on the other side of the world without you knowing about it, remind yourself that by travelling with your kids you've been teaching them about taking risks and making sensible choices. You can also help them prepare by talking through how they should deal with problems that might arise such as losing their passport, getting sick or injured or running out of money. Make sure they've got good medical and travel insurance, and have a chat about what level of communication you can both accept and adhere to. Be grateful we live in an age of smartphones and wi-fi where you will be able to have regular contact and see as well as hear what they are up to. But remember that this big trip is also an important part of your child (however old they are) becoming a fully fledged adult; being independent and free from the childhood home is key to that.

EXPLORE THEIR PASSIONS

Those who travel overseas often discover untapped passions they may not have come across otherwise. This may involve finding love for a new instrument, sport or art practice, or nurturing an interest in wildlife, food, fitness or photography. Travel also gives young adults the opportunity to better understand what they really enjoy and dislike before going into further study or down a career path. Travel itself can bring great clarity.

WATCH ATTITUDES SHIFT

Those small crises that would have once seemed like the end of the world for your child are likely to appear miniscule once they've faced adversities overseas. Life lessons gathered on the road hold huge weight, provoking reflection and making one appreciate the comforts of home. A little more gratitude isn't all too bad to acquire, either.

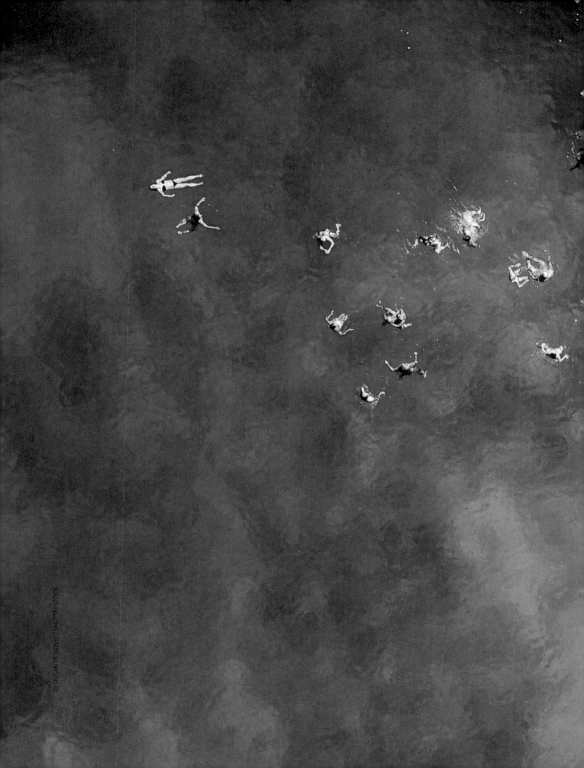

INSPIRATION

Family travel quiz

Not sure where to start your planning? Take our family traveller quiz to figure out the type of trip that's right for you.

1. You travel with your kids because...
a. You don't, the idea of it is too terrifying
b. It's good to get away
c. Travel teaches them so much
d. You want them to have a different perspective

2. Before you had kids, what was your travel style?
a. Happy to go most places but often with a tour operator
b. Spontaneous city breaks on a regular basis
c. Luxury all the way
d. Stretching out a trip for as long as financially possible

3. Thoughts on having a daily routine?
a. Ah, the security of stability
b. Love it but still count down to the holidays
c. Tolerate it while you plan your family's next adventure
d. Plan to ditch it and take the family around the world

4. What keeps you up at night when you think about taking your family on a trip?
a. Working out where would be a good place to go first
b. Health and safety concerns
c. Money
d. Working out where you can go next

5. What is your family's preferred method of transport?
a. Car
b. Plane
c. Train
d. All and any of the above as long as we're moving

6. How does your family handle the delays which inevitably occur when you travel?
a. By not travelling
b. By never leaving home without loads of snacks and a tablet
c. By embracing the challenge and working out a plan together
d. By taking delays in stride

7. How many bags do you travel with as a family?
a. However many you need to fit in the kitchen sink
b. Each person has their own suitcase
c. You're down to one shared bag and a cabin bag each
d. A backpack for each person

8. How does your family arrive at an airport?
a. You don't fly
b. On time with everything in the right bags
c. With your bikes ready to go cycling
d. With your enormous backpacks ready to go around the world

9. Your fellow passenger grimaces as you board with your babe-in-arms. Do you...
a. Turn tail and get off the plane
b. Start apologising profusely
c. Smile sweetly and offer to buy them a drink
d. Remind your child to kick the seat in front of them freely

10. Your kid has an accident or falls ill while you are on holiday. You...
a. Decide you are going home
b. Fly into a panic but then remember your first aid training
c. Tell them to pull themselves together
d. Calmly work out where the nearest doctor is and get them there

11. What's your family's idea of an adrenaline rush?
a. The swings and slides in the local park
b. Cycling downhill very fast
c. The fastest, scariest rollercoaster ride you can find
d. Floating over the Alps in a paraglider

12. Your kids prefer...
a. Theme parks
b. Museums
c. Water parks
d. Making friends with local kids

13. Which of these destinations is top of your family's bucket list?
a. Florida, USA
b. Brazil
c. Russia
d. India

14. What kind of souvenir is your family most likely to bring back from a trip?
a. A magnet
b. A piece of art
c. A new skill
d. You have no room for souvenirs, just incredible memories

15. What kind of travel experience excites you?
a. Trying local food
b. Doing something you wouldn't do at home
c. Have a proper conversation with a local
d. Arriving somewhere completely different

16. Which of these movies does your family love?
a. *Finding Nemo*
b. *Secret Life of Pets*
c. *Coco*
d. *Moana*

17. How do decisions get made in your family?
a. Very slowly and methodically
b. The children rule the roost
c. It's an absolutist state: the adults make the decisions
d. Democratically: everyone should have a say

18. What do you believe is the most important lesson children can learn from travel?
a. To read a map
b. How to communicate with people you don't know
c. How to take risks and learn from your mistakes
d. Flexibility, tolerance and understanding

Results

MOSTLY A – BEGIN WITH A STAYCATION

You want to explore the world more but the idea of taking your brood abroad is daunting. Make the most of opportunities in your area and start planning that camping trip in a local(ish) national park you've always talked about doing. If camping isn't your thing, book a rental place, pile everything in the car and just go. From little acorns do oak trees grow.

MOSTLY B – IT'S TIME TO SPREAD YOUR FAMILY'S TRAVEL WINGS

You are no longer taking baby travel steps, you're a fully fledged travelling toddler eager to plunge headfirst into new things. This could be your first trip abroad as a family, or your first time venturing to a mid- or long-haul destination. Don't run too fast though. Get personal recommendations, read family travel blogs and work out a trip which will be fun and with its challenges, but not too intense. After all, you're working on a lifelong love of travel for your family here.

MOSTLY C – YOUR FAMILY LOVES BEING ACTIVE SO START PLANNING THAT ADVENTURE

The kids are old enough now and you've done enough trips both domestically and internationally as a family that you are ready to take your family travel experiences to the next level. Sitting down with the kids and creating an itinerary around a specific activity or theme is a great start. But make sure you check out our list of ideas for adventures to really push the envelope.

MOSTLY D – YOUR FAMILY IS SO WELL TRAVELLED THAT YOU COULD WRITE A BLOG ON IT

You started small, you quickly went beyond your family's comfort zone and you now have loads of stories to tell from your adventures together. You are a fully paid-up member of the adventurous family travel club. But what's next? Go on, you know you want to! It's time to take to the road permanently and try life as a world nomad family.

After the trip

You did all your research and meticulously planned out the trip. You've been there, done it and now you've arrived back safe and sound with stories to tell, lessons learnt and the warm glow of time and money well invested in your family unit. But did you know that sharing and celebrating those memories you've worked so hard to create is also important? (Yes, the job of parenting really does never stop.)

Talking about the trip, creating visual reminders and regularly revisiting different elements of it cements the experience in the whole family's minds. Given that travel is such a huge learning opportunity, this is important for children's development. Remind them what they achieved while they were away and they can take the confidence gained from navigating a new culture or the creativity unleashed during a long boring car journey and bring it to their daily life and learning when back at home. This is especially relevant for children who have unique challenges. Knowing what they have achieved while travelling can help children with disabilities overcome other barriers they face.

Equally the bonds created by a family out exploring the world together, spending quality time with each other having fun and doing something different, will sustain everyone through the busy weeks when family members can seem like passing ships in the night. Memories made on family trips with grandparents or extended family are a rare commodity, to be cherished accordingly. Visual or verbal reminders of some of the fun, interesting or challenging things you achieved together on holiday play an important role in building those positive memories.

It's worth thinking how you want to remember the trip before you go so you can be prepared in terms of journals, sketch pads and so on and also allocating some time when you get home to create the visual reminders of your trip. Maybe you have a small fixed souvenir budget on trips to purchase items. In 20 years you will treasure the photos you spent time framing or laying out in an album or photobook.

Left: Taking a break at the Mayapan ruins in Mexico. Below: Put those family pictures into an album once you print them!

Photography on the road

We all know that recording an experience can help us remember it fondly and cherish the memories. Encourage your kids to keep their own diary or journal while you're away, or let them write postcards to family and friends with trip updates. Kids may want to take their own photos as well, especially now that they can be sent almost immediately to friends and family. Just don't get so wrapped up in documenting the trip that you start experiencing it at a remove!

Enjoy taking photographs of your children out and about exploring a new destination. Take loads as that way you have a greater chance of getting good ones, though don't always hide behind the lens either. Snaps or poses don't have to eat up huge amounts of the day or be a big deal. But remember to do some research on how photography is viewed in the destination you are visiting, and ask people's permission before you take their photo. For some cultures photography is not seen in a positive light, and everybody deserves the respect of being asked in advance if their photograph can be taken.

With the rise of the selfie culture it has become popular in some areas for locals to ask for selfies with travellers and especially so with children. Talk to your children about this before you start travelling, and agree how you want to approach it. Learning how to say no (or yes) nicely in the local language is a great tool for you all to have. And if using selfie sticks yourself, be extremely conscious of travellers around you. There's a reason many sites have now banned these contraptions, which can cause congestion at popular destinations.

DIFFERENT WAYS YOUR KIDS CAN CAPTURE LIFE ON THE ROAD

★

Carry a sketch pad and get the kids to draw what they see from time to time. It doesn't matter a jot if they are no budding Picasso. Whatever they draw will be priceless to you.

★

Find a children's book about your destination while you are travelling and take it home with you. It will serve as an excellent reminder of being somewhere different and learning what children there like to read.

★

Keep a simple travel journal. Just getting kids to draw, write or tell you one highlight of their day is a good way to start. You can supplement it with your photographs and anything else you've kept as a memento such as tickets and leaflets.

★

Use local postcards to note down what you've done each day and make them into a book when you get home.

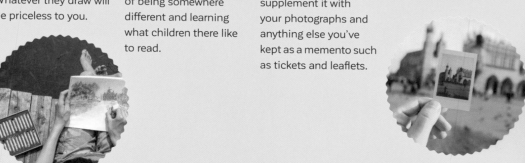

HOW TO MAKE THE MOST OF YOUR MILLIONS OF TRAVEL PHOTOGRAPHS

★

Don't leave them languishing on your phone or computer, print them out.

★

Pin or tape photos of where you have been together on a world map.

★

Frame them!

★

Take your favourite photos from the trip and turn them into notebooks, mugs or magnets. As the kids get older, these mementos are wonderful flashbacks to when they were taken.

★

Create a video using all your photographs, make a soundtrack using a song you listened to while you were away and watch it again and again.

★

Have a crafty session with your kids where they decorate some fun frames with whatever reminds them of your trip. Perfect for your holiday snaps!

★

Upload your digital photos to a digital frame that rotates through the pictures displayed.

★

Keep a chronological record of the trip, where you went, what you did, who you met and so on; you can use it when you look back at photographs later.

★

Get the children to save their pocket money or give them an allowance for the trip to spend on a souvenir for their bedroom when they get back home. Giving them the choice to decide, within reason, what they would like to remember the trip by is empowering and more likely to have a lasting impact.

★

As a family, choose a fridge magnet, mug or Christmas decoration from your destination. These visual references of where you have been as a family are a great way to get conversations going about the trips you have taken. Order something durable if your family is accident-prone!

Back home

Once home, don't just rush on with daily life and never look back. Photos, memorabilia or a bag of local sweets you brought back that everyone has to taste all serve an important purpose: to cement the experience, spark memories and build family bonds. You don't even need material things to start a conversation. A fun dinner table game can be to play 'guess where I am thinking of' and get the children to ask questions to work out which particular destination you have in mind.

Another great way to keep the vacation momentum rolling is to get your kids brainstorming your next trip. Maybe they are even old enough to do research or planning for the next adventure. It's also a great time to delve into any books or kids shows or

movies set in the region you've just returned from, or to start up those Spanish lessons you could have used abroad or practising tent set-up for backyard sleepovers. This is all part of setting your family's identity as one that travels together, and preparing your kids to be keen travellers later on, while appreciating the exploration of other cultures that can come at home without needing to go abroad chasing bucket list items.

© BLACK SALMON / SHUTTERSTOCK

© MARGARET.W / SHUTTERSTOCK

Left: A mother and daughter visiting the ruins at Angkor Wat, Cambodia. Below: Hiking by Mount Mitchell in the US.

TOP 10 FAMILY CULTURAL DESTINATIONS

Travel with your kids can broaden their understanding of other people and societies. Expand the whole family's cultural horizons on these inspiring trips.

1 OMAN

Elegant Muscat will give your kids an insight into a centuries-old way of life: join a dhow cruise or just sit and watch fishermen at work. Beyond the capital, there are mud-brick villages to explore, forts and castles to battle in, and souks where your kids can hone those haggling skills before rounding off the trip with some relaxing time at the beach.

2 NORWAY

Get an insight into Scandinavian culture with Viking museums, theme parks with trolls and fairy palaces, elk safaris and dogsledding. Norway is also increasingly popular for families introducing their children to that popular Nordic activity: skiing.

© KENNETH SCHOTH / 500PX

3 EMILIA-ROMAGNA, ITALY

There's Parma ham and parmesan for your little foodies, the mosaics of Ravenna for budding artists and photogenic Bologna, which has a past to fascinate history buffs. And that's not to leave out beach culture in Rimini, more incredible art in Ferrara and the Unesco World Heritage site of Modena's cathedral.

4 ORKNEY, SCOTLAND

The adventurous journey required to reach Orkney will kick-start your family's immersion into the islands' fascinating cultural heritage. Once off the ferry you have 5000 years of history to explore, from the ruins of a Neolithic village at Skara Brae and the Viking legacy at Kirkwall to the role played by Orkney in World War II, which is well documented at the Scapa Flow Visitor Centre.

© MATT MUNRO / LONELY PLANET

5 AMSTERDAM, THE NETHERLANDS

You can do serious science at the hands-on NEMO Museum, serious art (the Rijksmuseum has excellent family tours) and even more serious history: the Anne Frank House needs no introduction and, at the Verzetsmuseum Junior, you can learn the stories of four Dutch children during the occupation. But when it's time to have fun you can also take a pedal boat on the canals and eat stacks of delicious Dutch pancakes.

6 NASHVILLE, TENNESSEE, USA

Could there be a better way to introduce your family to country-music culture than a weekend in Nashville? The Country Music Hall of Fame has interactive exhibits, listening booths and the chance to make your own song as a family; the Johnny Cash Museum has films to keep little ones engaged; and lastly, kids love seeing the city with the Music City Hop-On Hop-Off Trolley.

7 BRISBANE, AUSTRALIA

Start with Aboriginal art in the Queensland Art Gallery and Gallery of Modern Art (QAGOMA), which runs sessions for children. Then splash around on man-made Streets Beach (perfect for small swimmers) or let off steam in the tree-house playground at New Farm Park. Relax with a BBQ in the riverside South Bank Parklands before checking out koalas at nearby Lone Pine Koala Sanctuary. All in all, a quintessential Australian experience.

8 KYOTO, JAPAN

A visit to Kyoto is a great first step for Western kids to understand Japanese culture, as there are plenty of distractions if the cultural overload is too much. Take Fushimi Inari Taisha with its famous torii gates: it's a fascinating example of a traditional shrine, but there's space to burn off energy. Or the Shōren-in temple, which has carp to count and a bamboo forest to explore in its landscaped gardens.

9 ST PETERSBURG, RUSSIA

With plenty of fun activities and good restaurants for kids, St Petersburg is a gentle introduction to Russian culture. The Zoological Museum is one of a number of interesting attractions, there are traditional puppet and circus shows to watch and you can even book onto a workshop to paint your own *matryoshka* (wooden nesting doll).

10 RAJASTHAN, INDIA

This is the India of storybooks: medieval forts, fairy-tale palaces, vibrant festivals, tiger safaris, and all against the backdrop of a well-oiled tourist infrastructure so you can book family-friendly tours and accommodations to suit all of you.

© MATT MUNRO / LONELY PLANET

TOP 5

DESTINATIONS FOR INFANTS & TODDLERS

While the world is pretty much your oyster when it comes to travel with very small people, these destinations suit families with younger children best.

© JONATHAN STOKES / LONELY PLANET

2 **SICILY, ITALY —** Family life is highly valued in Sicily. Babies are cooed over, breastfeeding in public is common and children of all ages are welcomed at restaurants, historical sites and village markets. For toddlers there's plenty of relaxed fun on the sandy beaches, roaming round ancient ruins or joining the evening *passeggiata*.

3 **SUNSHINE COAST, AUSTRALIA —** Home to flawless beaches, a range of coastal resort towns with their own appeal and vibe, plenty of family-friendly accommodation options and comfortably warm temperatures. You can see why we're recommending the Sunshine Coast! Just pick one base to keep driving time reasonable.

4 **DEVON & CORNWALL, UK —** The southwest corner of the UK is home to plenty of National Trust properties, which usually provide gardens for energetic toddlers to run around and a lovely tea room to revive sleep-deprived new parents. It's also a beautiful part of the world with many family-friendly places to stay so you can rest in comfort.

© STUART WESTMORLAND / GETTY IMAGES

1 **SAN DIEGO, USA —** With its mild marine climate and its beach city vibe, San Diego is a good place for families with babes in arms to wander around. It also caters perfectly to the toddler crowd with its famous zoo, an aquarium and now the New Children's Museum as well as plazas, fountains and gardens to let off steam.

5 **MALDIVES —** Typically associated with honeymooners, a family-friendly resort in the Maldives can work perfectly for very young children due to the relaxed pace of life, the chance to play in the natural world, and the fact that parents can escape distractions.

© MATTEO COLOMBO / GETTY IMAGES

TOP 5

DESTINATIONS FOR PRIMARY OR ELEMENTARY SCHOOL-AGE KIDS

Plan your trips around what the kids are learning at school for the most enriching trip.

© GUILLAUME BURET / 500PX

2 GREECE — Whether it's from the curriculum or from the Rick Riordan books on Percy Jackson, you can bring the stories of ancient Greece to life with a trip combining Athens and some of the islands. The added bonus is that you will enjoy great food, lovely beaches and the famous Mediterranean welcome for families.

3 DENMARK — A place so child-friendly it even has a 'Capital of Children'. This kid-friendly utopia is centred on Billund, the heartland of Lego, but around it there are plenty of other attractions too, including a Viking town, Scandinavia's best water park and the fantastic Givskud Zoo.

4 MEXICO CITY AND THE YUCATÁN — The sights, sounds and colours of Mexico excite kids, and it's a family-friendly culture. Learn about ancient Mayan and Aztec culture through some excellent child-focused museums as well as the pyramids themselves, but also have lots of fun on the beach.

© ENRIQUE RAMOS LOPEZ / 500PX

1 CANADA — Between wildlife sightings, cowboy encounters, hands-on pirate history, hunting for dinosaur fossils and ice-skating on mountain lakes, there is so much to keep younger children engaged across Canada.

5 CAPPADOCIA, TURKEY — Famous for the spectacular hot-air balloon rides which are adventure enough, the honeycombed hills and conical rock formations of Cappadocia will make any child's imagination run wild. Underground cities offer an extra thrill.

© MARK READ / LONELY PLANET

TOP 5

DESTINATIONS FOR TWEENS & TEENS

Get older children excited by factoring in their personal interests, finding an adrenaline hit or taking them to a destination which their peers love.

1 BERLIN, GERMANY

Berlin is both glamorous and gritty, with a vibrant culture, cutting-edge architecture, fabulous food and tangible history. There's so much for tweens and teens to get their teeth into here.

© TURTIX / SHUTTERSTOCK

2 JASPER NATIONAL PARK, CANADA

The Rockies are the perfect backdrop to get your reluctant teens engaged in some serious activities. While skiing or hiking are obvious options, depending on the season you can also take out mountain bikes or try fat-biking through the snow. Half their friends won't even know what fat-biking is, so that's a great story to take home.

3 AUCKLAND, NEW ZEALAND

You may think of Queenstown as the adventure capital of New Zealand, but the area in and around Auckland is a great alternative for families with teenagers. There are plenty of ways to get some thrills (try land-yachting, canyoning and the infamous bungee jump – age restrictions apply) as well as some great restaurants, museums and galleries.

4 CUBA

Taking your teens somewhere culturally different can kick-start their engagement in the family trip. Cuba's revolutionary history, its vibrant music scene, the laid-back vibe and the beautiful beaches are all reasons the country appeals to teens. Step away from the resorts and get off the beaten track to open your children's eyes to the challenges and rewards of independent travel.

5 DUBAI, UAE

There are huge malls for shopping, loads of theme parks, gaming zones, beaches to chill out on and then there's the desert to have some fun in a 4x4. Seriously, show us a tween or teen who wouldn't be happy in Dubai.

© TOMASZ GANCLERZ / SHUTTERSTOCK

TOP 5

DESTINATIONS FOR MULTI-GENERATIONAL TRAVEL

If you are travelling with three generations (or more) you'll want destinations with something for all.

1 YELLOWSTONE NATIONAL PARK, US

From seeing the famous Grand Prismatic Spring to watching Old Faithful erupt, following bison through your binoculars and then taking a hike together, there's plenty to keep a multigenerational group occupied and interested in Yellowstone. Research how to get off the popular routes to avoid the crowds.

2 CAPE TOWN & THE WINELANDS, SOUTH AFRICA

This is a beautiful part of the world with a family-friendly climate and plenty for all ages to enjoy; start with a few leisurely days exploring Cape Town (everyone will love the view from Table Mountain and the penguins at Boulders Beach) and then head out to visit animal reserves and vineyards, some of which have restaurants attached and space for kids to run around.

3 BUDAPEST, HUNGARY

Easy to navigate and explore, Budapest is a good option for a city break with a larger group of different ages. Come in the summer to make the most of the thermal baths and pools which everyone will love. There's also plenty of live entertainment, some good museums and an excellent coffee and cake scene. Any transport enthusiasts in your party will also be in seventh heaven.

4 THE DORDOGNE, FRANCE

Less well known than Provence or the Loire, the Dordogne boasts many excellent accommodation options for larger family groups plus a wealth of activities to keep the young and the young at heart happy. You can visit prehistoric caves, explore castles, meander through markets, take a canoe down the river, hire bikes, tour vineyards or just enjoy a long lunch while the kids play in the local square.

5 TASMANIA, AUSTRALIA

Tasmania is a naturally active destination, with plenty of opportunities for everyone to get involved and no huge distances to cover in between. When a gentler pace is needed there are restaurants with superb local cuisine, wildlife parks to learn about indigenous creatures such as wombats and the chance to do some serious stargazing all together.

TOP 10
SCIENCE DESTINATIONS

If your children are keen to explore the world of science here's where they can geek out.

1. STARGAZE IN CHILE'S ATACAMA DESERT —
Thanks to cloudless skies and virtually no light pollution, Earth's driest non-polar desert is the ultimate stargazing spot. It's home to the aptly-named Valley of the Moon and some of the world's top observatories. Child-friendly tours take in the night sky with a 70cm telescope.

2. ÞINGVELLIR NATIONAL PARK, ICELAND —
The whole of Iceland is an adventure for kids, with its wide-open spaces, wildlife and science projects brought to life. Budding geologists will be fascinated by Þingvellir National Park, a fissured rift valley where the North American and Eurasian tectonic plates meet.

3. WATCH THE NORTHERN LIGHTS IN SWEDISH LAPLAND —
Pack warmly and head to the Swedish village of Abisko, where a chairlift goes up to the Aurora Sky Station, renowned as the world's best place to view the Northern Lights. Look up in awe, or delve deeper into the phenomenon with a guided station tour.

4. ACT LIKE AN ASTRONAUT IN FLORIDA, US —
With real-life rocket launches, Florida's Kennedy Space Center is guaranteed to get kids starry-eyed. They can complete NASA-science-based challenges (build a habitat on Mars! Save Earth from an asteroid!) to score a Commander's Badge at the interactive Cosmic Quest; pilot a space shuttle in an astronaut training simulator; crawl through a space station model; and whoosh off into orbit on the Shuttle Launch Experience.

5. STARGAZE AT NAGOYA CITY SCIENCE MUSEUM PLANETARIUM, JAPAN —
Housed in a gigantic silver globe, the world's biggest planetarium projects the exact positions of over 9000 stars in astonishing detail across its dome.

Kid-centric programmes are aligned with current astronomical events including eclipses and meteorite showers, and there are shows on constellations, space travel and more.

6. DIG UP A DINOSAUR AT THE WYOMING DINOSAUR CENTRE, THERMOPOLIS, US — Seventh

heaven for young (and old) paleontologists. The collection of fossils is incredible and regularly listed as one of the top ten dinosaur museums in the world, but the real show stealer is the Kids Dig Program where children age eight to 12 experience a full day of digging, prepping and casting. If they find a fossil they learn how to preserve and record it, and everyone gets to make a cast of a fossil which they then take home. And, yes, there is an adult version too.

7. DIVE INTO THE NATURAL WORLD AT COSMOCAIXA IN BARCELONA —

'Touch' is the order of the day inside this hands-on natural science museum, with exhibits that include an Amazonian rainforest complete with crocodiles and live piranhas and a 'geological wall' made of real rock. Try an experiment or two in the family science lab.

8. TOUR THE HADRON COLLIDER, CERN, SWITZERLAND — Your budding

physicist or chemist will be buzzing with new knowledge at the end of this tour. As well as the guided tour which takes you behind the scenes (but doesn't show you the actual collider), there is a multimedia exhibition to learn about how the collider works and what life is like for Cern scientists.

9. QUESTION EVERYTHING AT QUESTACON IN CANBERRA, AUSTRALIA —

The National Science and Technology Centre is a hive of activity and perfect for small people with lots of questions to ask. Tiny hands can manipulate experiments, including an earthquake simulator, a giant free-fall slide and an air-hockey robot waiting for its next challenger. Mini-scientists aged six and under are catered for with their own zone.

10. PLAY AT THE ARTSCIENCE MUSEUM, SINGAPORE — This interactive

space will captivate adults and children alike. Stand under a digital waterfall, watch your children's sea creature designs swim in a digital aquarium and let the kids throw themselves into an enormous pit of glowing balls that change colour when bumped.

TOP 10
DESTINATIONS WITH A DIFFERENCE

If your family is ready to take on a challenge it's time to consider some destinations you might previously have ruled out.

© IMAGESEF / SHUTTERSTOCK

1 LANZAROTE, CANARY ISLANDS, SPAIN — César Manrique's mesmerising works provide a fantasy voyage for children and a cultural fix for adults, plus there's the eerie landscape of Timanfaya National Park, world-class surfing and some steep but deserted cycling roads.

2 DENMARK — The immense Legoland perhaps has pride of place, but you can also explore Copenhagen's Little Mermaid statue in honour of Hans Christian Andersen and check out the Viking artifacts in Ribe. Summer days are exceedingly long, leaving ample time to explore.

© IMAGESEF / SHUTTERSTOCK

3 LOFOTEN ISLANDS, NORWAY — Outdoor adventure is a given here and as the islands lie inside the Arctic Circle you'll enjoy incredibly long summer days to explore the traditional villages, take boat trips up narrow fjords, visit bird and seal colonies, discover a Viking longhouse or wander around artists' galleries.

4 GOBI DESERT, MONGOLIA — This vast landscape doesn't often feature in recommendations for family travel, but if you enjoy wild open spaces and the whiff of adventure, you can stay with nomadic tribes in *ger* camps, see dramatic ice canyons and spectacular dunes, and visit one of the world's largest dinosaur graveyards at the cliffs of Bayanzag.

© KARWISCH.DE / 500PX

5 LAKE MALAWI, MALAWI — There are few formal facilities for children in Malawi; however, the country is generally a safe and friendly place for children to visit. Older kids will love the outdoor activities that Malawi has to offer, and many lodges in the wilderness areas and beaches are geared towards families.

© MARK READ / LONELY PLANET

6 WORKING RANCH HOLIDAYS, USA –

Introduce your family to big skies, dramatic scenery and plenty of time in the saddle. You can learn to ride or improve your skills, take on some rodeo training or trek high into the hills. By night you can learn to line dance.

7 HERM, THE CHANNEL ISLANDS, GREAT BRITAIN – Remote yet

accessible, exotic yet affordable, diminutive Herm was made for old-fashioned adventure. There are no cars or even bikes here, and kids can enjoy that increasingly rare pleasure of complete freedom. Stay in a pre-pitched tent at the Seagull campsite for instant buddies, explore the beaches, rock pools and coastal paths, and discover mysterious Neolithic tombs.

8 MARDI GRAS, NEW ORLEANS, USA

– Ignore your preconceptions, go beyond the boozy Bourbon Street festivities and take your kids on an adventure in this most famous of parades. Kids can snag 'throws' – the fun trinkets and goodies tossed out.

© SIOUXSNAPP / SHUTTERSTOCK

9 SWAKOPMUND, NAMIBIA –

Known for its adrenaline-inducing sports, Swakopmund is the perfect base for adding some thrills to your African trip. Your family can try sandboarding, skydiving, quad biking, sailing, surfing, kayaking and fishing. Then head to Sossusvlei, for some desert camping and the chance to learn all about life in the dry lands.

© MARK HANNAFORD / GETTY IMAGES

© LIUFUYU / GETTY IMAGES

10 YANGSHUO, CHINA – For

many families the experience of visiting anywhere in China is a cultural adventure, but in the Yangshuo region you can add a physical dimension. Go cycling, rock-climbing and river-cruising all against the most incredible scenic backdrop.

TOP 10
POP CULTURE DESTINATIONS

Many a film or book has taken inspiration from a particular landscape or specific part of the world, so why not take your own inspiration for your next trip from one of these classic family-friendly movies or works of children's literature?

1 MEET MOANA

Make your way to the South Pacific to visit the region portrayed in *Moana*. The pristine Teti'aroa atoll, with its enclosed lagoon, was the likely inspiration for Motonui, while Bora Bora's Mount Otemanu is also reminiscent of the fictional island. For a taste of South Pacific hospitality, visit family-friendly Fiji or Aulani, a Disney resort on the Hawaiian island of Oahu, where Moana herself entertains guests with storytelling and hands-on activities.

2 ADVENTURES WITH KING ARTHUR

While nobody knows if there really was a King Arthur, Wales' claim to being the birthplace of Arthurian legend is convincing thanks to locations like Caerleon, cited as the setting for Camelot by Geoffrey of Monmouth. Warm up for the journey by reading TH White's *The Once and Future King*, which tracks the legendary king through knight-training school, and hike to the summit of Snowdon, where Arthur reputedly killed a giant.

3 TOUR TOVE JANSSON'S MOOMINLAND

Their creator was a Finn, and the islands that dot the Gulf of Finland were the inspiration for the magical glades where Moomintroll cavorted with Snufkin and Snorkmaiden. Set the scene with *The Moomins and the Great Flood*, then take the kids to the real Moominvalley by renting a mökki (cottage) on the Pellinki Islands near Porvoo. For a more commercial alternative, visit Moominworld in Naantali.

4 FLAP, FLUTTER AND FLY TO RIO

Fans of Blu the macaw from the film *Rio* should travel, logically enough, to Rio de Janeiro. Blu is based on the Spix's macaw, a critically endangered species thought to be extinct in the wild. So while you won't find Blu in Rio, families can still spot some others of Brazil's 1800 bird species. Either head into the Amazon jungle or get up close to 140 bird species plus wild monkeys and marmosets at Rio's Botanical Garden.

5 RATATOUILLE IN PARIS

Swing by La Tour d'Argent, the inspiration for fictional restaurant Gusteau's, then stroll the Seine. Visit Musée des Égouts, the museum devoted to sewers, and dine at Disneyland Paris' Bistrot Chez Rémy.

6 DIGGING FOR TREASURE ISLAND

The Caribbean is rarely a tough sell for beach-loving kids, but why not up the ante with a few chapters of *Treasure Island*? The true setting for Robert Louis Stevenson's genre-defining pirate epic is hotly disputed, but Norman Island in the British Virgin Islands and Isla del Coco off Costa Rica are both strong candidates. Tell them there's treasure under that golden sand and they'll be digging for hours while you relax with a rum punch.

7 LONDON: A BEARY NICE TOWN TO VISIT

It's easy to find traces of Peru-born Paddington Bear all over London. Start with Paddington station, where you'll find a bronze statue of the polite bear ready for his close-up, as well as a Paddington Shop. Plenty of London landmarks feature in the Paddington films, including Serpentine Lake, St Paul's Cathedral, the Shard and Buckingham Palace. Don't forget to pack some marmalade sandwiches under your hat.

8 MEETING MOWGLI IN INDIA

Think about *The Jungle Book* and you'll soon be humming tunes from the Disney cartoon, but Rudyard Kipling's original is the best primer for a trip to the Indian jungle. Ranthambhore National Park in Rajasthan is the ideal stand-in for the steamy forests where Mowgli and Baloo gambolled – you might even spot a real Baloo, alongside tigers and leopards.

9 TREKKING WITH TINTIN

A romp spanning the Himalayas, *Tintin in Tibet* serves up sacred mountains, levitating monks and even the odd yeti. You have a chance of spotting all three along the trekking route to Everest Base Camp, though yeti sightings may be restricted to body parts preserved in mountain monasteries. Consider hiring a porter to help carry younger trekkers when little legs get tired.

10 LIVE THE DAY OF THE DEAD WITH COCO

Picturesque colonial town Santa Fe de la Laguna in the Michoacán region was the inspiration behind the Rivera family's hometown. To explore a Land of the Dead landscape, journey to the historic centre of Mexico City.

TOP 10
FUN IDEAS

Take your kids on an amazing adventure to these inventive ideas, and brainstorm your own offbeat activities.

1. HAVE A SLEEPOVER WITH A DIFFERENCE — Imagine exploring our planet's rich history, diving deep to the bottom of the ocean, discovering what other galaxies look like and learning all about our furry friends at night, when all the other visitors have gone home. It's a truly incredible experience and one your kids can do at any number of museums, galleries, aquariums or zoos around the world.

2. FIND SECRET SWIMMING POOLS —
Mexico's Yucatán Peninsula is home to thousands of cenotes – natural freshwater swimming holes formed by the collapse of porous limestone bedrock. Some are cavernous, others are lit by shafts of light from the jungle canopy above. Combining bright turquoise water and the thrill of finding something so unusual, swimming in a cenote is usually a big hit with kids.

3. GET CREATIVE WITH CLAY — If your creative child is ready to make the jump from mud pies to something a bit more advanced, it's time to take the pottery wheel for a spin. Held just down the road from one of the world's great masterpieces – Angkor Wat – Siem Reap's ceramics workshops help pint-sized potters create their very own Angkor-inspired bowl, complete with Khmer flower carvings. You'll get the clay out from their fingernails eventually, but mucky memories – and an impressive 'potter's diploma' – will last forever.

4. TURN YOUR EYES TO THE SKY — To check out your nearest dark sky site, pack some blankets, plenty of snacks and a flask of hot chocolate. Arm the kids with binoculars or a telescope and if boredom kicks in encourage them to make up their own constellations.

5. NURTURE GREEN THUMBS — Plant, paddle and play dirty in Melbourne at the

© ELZBIETA SEKOWSKA / SHUTTERSTOCK

Royal Botanic Gardens' famously hands-on Ian Potter Foundation Children's Garden. Educational and inclusive, the huge garden is packed with interactive places for kids of all ages to explore. Clamber under rocks in the Ruin Garden, make a splash in the water spout and go bug-hunting in the Wetlands pond. Aspiring agriculturalists (or anyone who just loves dirt) will dig the Kitchen Garden.

6. RIDE THE RAILS —

Taking a night train turns the journey into an adventure involving new cities, a comfy cabin and novelty sleeping arrangements. Children squeal at the fact seats turn into cosy beds; revel at the chance to eat meals 'on wheels'; and soon master the art of scenery spotting without sticking their heads out of the windows. The Ghan in Australia whizzes you across a continent overnight; and the Caledonian Sleeper transports the whole family from busy London to scenic Scotland in style, but there are plenty more to choose from.

7. LOOK AFTER ELEPHANTS — There

are plenty of animal sanctuaries happy to take children as volunteers, but the Elephant Hills in Thailand's Khao Sok National Park is a pretty special experience. There's loads to explore in the park and you stay in a luxury tented camp, but the highlight is getting to bathe, feed and spend quality time with rescued elephants.

8. STEP BACK IN TIME FOR THE DAY —

Bring history to life with a gladiator training session at Rome's Colosseum, complete with swords, tunics and instructions on the gladiatorial games. In a similar vein you can be a knight at Warwick Castle in England or a spy at Washington, DC's International Spy Museum.

9. TRAIN UP A SOUS CHEF — Family

cooking courses are a brilliant way to encourage fussy eaters, teach children about the local cuisine and bond together as a family as you learn something new. Try making pizza in Naples, tagine in Morocco or pho in Vietnam. You may unleash a love of cooking in the kids.

10. EMBRACE PARKS — Whether it's a

world-class theme park, fun-filled water park or simply a lovely local playground, kids of all ages love parks. If going to a huge amusement park, just be sure to pace yourselves.

TOP 5
BUDGET DESTINATIONS FOR FAMILIES

Try visiting these incredible family-friendly landscapes, achievable without breaking the bank.

© ROLAND BARAT / 500PX

2 **SLOVENIA —** This pocket of Europe in miniature will give you a city break in a relaxed capital, Venetian-influenced seaside towns and small villages to explore, but what really makes it affordable is the alpine adventures you can have (in both summer and winter) without breaking the bank.

3 **SRI LANKA —** This island in the Indian Ocean is putting its past behind it and proving to be an affordable destination for families seeking out adventure, despite the attacks of 2019. Think rickshaws and rickety old trains to ride, tea plantations to explore and beaches to frolic on. Public transport and guest houses are good values.

4 **ECUADOR —** A relatively compact place to travel around, there are many ways you can budget carefully in Ecuador. The Galápagos may be wallet-busting but there's plenty else to explore if you avoid the islands: postcard-pretty colonial centres, white-sand beaches, Kichwa villages, Amazonian rainforest and the breathtaking Andes.

©MARK READ / LONELY PLANET

1 **CAMPSITES IN US NATIONAL PARKS —** Make your reservations far in advance, then sit back and enjoy the park of your choice in all its glory. Wake up to a dewy sunrise for much less than you would spend in a hotel. The www.nps.gov site has a dedicated section on camping and a page of tips on camping with your kids.

5 **LAZIO, ITALY —** Central Italy, including Rome (which is a chaotic, fun, fascinating and good value city break with kids), has plenty to explore with its palazzos, sweet hillside villages and lakes to cool off in, at lower prices than Tuscany or Umbria.

© DANIELE DE RUBEIS / 500PX

TOP 5
FAMILY-FRIENDLY CRUISES

Megaships have plenty to keep kids occupied at sea. Think Disney cruises, kids clubs, amazing pools and all the fun you can have on board and in port.

© PICS721 / SHUTTERSTOCK

2 BAHAMAS — If you are touching land anywhere near Paradise Island, head straight to Atlantis, where daytrippers can purchase a pass to its massive water park facility that fuses together kid fun such as waterslides and over-water jungle gyms with plenty of amenities.

3 TAURANGA — There's something for every interest in New Zealand's Bay of Plenty. Any *Lords of the Rings* fans in the family will love seeing the Hobbiton set at Tauranga. Visit Māori villages to learn about the culture of the country's original residents, and go to Rotorua to be awed by incredible geothermal activity.

4 HAWAII — Hang ten along the shores of the Aloha State, where you can snorkel with turtles, try a surfing tutorial or let your curious kids engage in cultural traditions, thoughtfully distilled into colourful classes taught by local ambassadors.

© EMPERORCOSAR / SHUTTERSTOCK

1 ST THOMAS — There's probably no island in the Caribbean that packs more activities onto its shores than this one. Try zip-lining and parasailing, or take the Skyride gondola to Paradise Point. Day passes to some of the island's hotels are available too, so you can give yourselves a change of scene.

5 ALASKA — Itineraries are very much geared to those with kids thanks to tons of active excursions. You can take a floatplane, go bear-spotting, hike a glacier, visit a dog musher's camp, watch whales, learn to kayak —and the list goes on!

© KEN BALDWIN / 500PX

TOP 5

BEACH DESTINATIONS

Look for protected bays, gentle waves, a gradual shore and ideally a lifeguard (although nothing can replace parental supervision) at these kid-friendly beaches.

1 SURFSIDE BEACH, SOUTH CAROLINA

With its long-established reputation as a family-friendly beach, this beach town is now also the first certified autism-friendly destination in the world (meaning that staff at most local attractions have been trained and certified by the Champion Autism Network). There's also wheelchair access to the beach and Myrtle Beach Boardwalk only 15 minutes away for some fairground fun.

2 OKINAWA & THE SOUTHWEST ISLANDS, JAPAN

Take your family well and truly off the beaten track to this popular destination for local families. Centred on a flower-decorated village of traditional houses, life on Taketomi is simple. There are no cars, not much after-dark entertainment and low-key beaches. Perfect for families wanting to unwind together.

3 CYLINDER BEACH, STRADBROKE ISLAND, AUSTRALIA

This broad, beautiful Queensland beach is patrolled by lifesavers, offers easy access from the car park and generally has smaller waves than neighbouring beaches. It's also a hot spot for spying dolphins, turtles, manta rays and, between June and November, humpback whales.

4 BARMOUTH, SNOWDONIA, WALES

A lovely and clean Blue Flag beach has plenty of space to build sandcastles and go rock-pooling. It's also home to a typical British seaside resort so you can get fish and chips when the kids are getting hungry.

© 2016, VISIT WALES

5 PUNTA ESMERALDA, MEXICO

This completely open freshwater cenote is crystal clear and looks like a natural splash pool, the perfect place for babies and toddlers to cool off. If you look hard enough you can spot the water bubbling up from the underwater river system. The white-sand beach also has a playground area with slides and monkey bars, and there's a deck for wheelchair access.

TOP 5

WILDLIFE HOLIDAYS

Use local guides, binoculars and reference books to spot the best wildlife at these nature-rich destinations.

1 NAMIBIA

Hire a car and take your family on a self-drive safari through Etosha National Park; it's easy to see the animals, there are plenty of camps to get out and stretch legs, and the distances are manageable.

© LUCA ROGGERO / GETTY IMAGES

2 COSTA RICA

You can't fail to spot wildlife in Costa Rica: stay a day or two in a jungle lodge and the wildlife will come to you. This small peaceful country also has all the amenities that appeal to parents.

© ONDREJ PROSICKY / SHUTTERSTOCK

3 GALÁPAGOS ISLANDS, ECUADOR

These islands are a well-known paradise for animal lovers, as there's so much to see and learn about. They are accessible to families either by booking on family-friendly ships or taking a land-based trip which gives you time at the beach.

© DC_COLOMBIA / GETTY IMAGES

3 GREAT BARRIER REEF, AUSTRALIA

No explanation needed here, just your snorkels and masks (or if your kids are older than 12 you can try scuba diving). There's a plethora of family-friendly resorts and islands to choose from as well as plenty of options for glass-bottomed boats, submerged viewing platforms and reef walks to suit all families. Make sure to bring reef-appropriate biodegradable sun protection.

4 KANHA NATIONAL PARK, INDIA

Madhya Pradesh is home to healthy populations of Bengal tigers, langur monkeys, swamp deer and antelope. It provides an exhilarating destination for 4WD jeep tours or guided walks. Once you've had your fill of wildlife, the Taj Mahal, colourful Jaipur and the temples of Khajuraho are within easy reach.

DAVID ELSE, LONELY PLANET WRITER

From left:
Riding horses
in Drakensberg;
crocodile crossing.

South Africa & eSwatini safari

What's it like to travel here as a family?

South Africa and eSwatini (previously Swaziland) are home to huge national parks and wilderness areas, which satisfied our family's desire to enjoy the natural sights and sounds of the continent – red earth, yellow acacias, chirping cicadas, grunting hippos. They also have great historical sites, plentiful tourism facilities, easy-to-drive roads and well-stocked shops.

Tell us your favourite parts of the trip.

We landed at Johannesburg, picked up a rental car, and our first stop was the Cradle of Humankind, one of the world's most important regions for hominid fossil discoveries. The Maropeng museum provided a great mix of hands-on activities for kids and informative exhibits for grown-ups, while the deep cave at Sterkfontein was enthralling for everyone.

Preferring to remain outside the city, we checked into Kenjara Lodge, a quirky little hotel with thatched cottages in the garden – ideal family accommodation. On the edge of the garden was an easy-to-climb tree and a boulder pile where the kids played for hours in the sunshine while we sat on the veranda with binoculars, bird books and cold beers.

Next was the Drakensberg, a vast mountain range that separates South Africa from Lesotho, the independent kingdom next door. A mountain road wound up to the sleepy town of Underberg and long time backpackers' favourite Khotso. Eschewing the dorms, we opted for family rooms but enjoyed the communal atmosphere and chatting to other travellers about their journeys, while the kids played happily outside. There are great walks in the foothills, but even better was a horse trek up to the higher ground. The local Basuto ponies were patient and sure-footed, so perfect for children.

Thick coats were swapped for swimsuits as our next stop was the Indian Ocean at St Lucia, a relaxed little resort town. For families, this place had everything: great beaches for swimming and snorkelling and iSimangaliso Wetland Park, a vast area of coast, dunes, lakes, forest and grassland.

FAMILY TRAVEL HANDBOOK

Highlights at iSimangaliso included a boat ride with up-close hippo and croc encounters, a wildlife safari with sightings of rhinos and a day at Cape Vidal that none of us will ever forget. We sat on silver-white sands, while monkeys scrambled in the trees above the dunes. In front, our kids paddled in the shallow waves, while beyond them humpback whales breached above the surface and then fell back into the water with a giant splash.

How about challenges?

Importantly, we wanted to introduce our children Sarah (age 10) and Michael (age 8) to travelling, and to give them a chance to see a positive side of Africa, one not often portrayed in today's media. And because it had been 15 years since my wife and I had travelled in Africa ourselves, a road trip was perfect for rekindling old memories. Don't overestimate the obstacles!

Any words of advice?

Numerous airlines serve South Africa. The total flying time from the UK was about 12 hours each way. The kids breezed through the flights, thanks largely to the seat-back video screens. We travelled by rental car, and all the usual international brands are found in South Africa. A great car choice for families is the Nissan Qashqai or the Hyundai ix35. Both SUVs, they provide enough room for a family of four. Being higher than a normal sedan/saloon car, they are better for viewing animals. We stayed in some hotels, and mainly provided our own meals. Shopping for supplies along the way was straightforward.

Who's it for?

Throughout the journey, we all enjoyed adventurous activities and simply being in Africa, without the kids feeling uncomfortable or too far beyond the familiar. For us, South Africa and Swaziland provided a perfect family holiday, and we're already planning the next adventure there.

What are the kid-friendly experiences to seek out?

Wildlife was easy to see at Mlilwane Wildlife Sanctuary in Swaziland. Impala wandered past the window of our quaint colonial-style bungalow, while a warthog family slept in the dust nearby. Thanks to the lack of lions and other dangerous beasts, Mlilwane offers horseback safaris that allowed us to get almost within touching distance of zebra.

Our final stop was beautiful Malolotja, popular for wilderness hiking although our own walks were on the short side due to little legs and a nearby boulder field where every giant rock needed to be climbed. Malolotja also has a Canopy Tour of zip-wires between airy platforms, zigzagging high above a dramatic tree-filled canyon.

Clockwise from top left: South Africa's coastline; Drakensberg mountains; a hippo on safari; exploring the ropes course.

COURTESY OF DAVID ELSE

COURTESY OF SHOBHA GEORGE

Brazil Carnival

From left: An ornate carnival
float; getting silly in Rio.

What's it like to travel here as a family?

With a vacation in Rio de Janeiro at Carnival time, you get a beach holiday that is the setting for one of the biggest festivals in the world! The music, dancing and infectious joy of Carnival in Rio is an unforgettable experience.

Tell us your favourite parts of the trip.

During Carnival people from all walks of life in Rio de Janeiro come together to celebrate in a festival which ushers in the Catholic season of Lent. Cariocas (as the locals call themselves) forget about their problems for a few days of intense partying and parades.

Undoubtedly, the best attraction in Rio is its wide strip of white sand beach hugging the Atlantic Ocean. You can spend the entire day at the beach and the adjoining boardwalk and never get bored. Cariocas love their beaches and with good reason. Among the things to do are people watching, soaking in the sunshine, playing in the waves and catching the beautiful sunsets.

Copacabana, Ipanema and Leblon beaches are all neighbouring beaches separated by Postos (numbered lifeguard areas). Ipanema and Leblon beaches are the most popular with families. Use the Postos to orient yourself if you decide to take a walk along the boardwalk to see the vendors peddling their wares and refresh yourself with water from freshly cut coconuts.

Overlooking the city, the Christ the Redeemer statue was completed in 1931 to commemorate Brazilian independence from Portugal. The best way to get to the statue is the Corcovado Cog Train which in itself is a part of Brazil's history, having been inaugurated in 1884. A cable car ride up to the top of Sugarloaf Mountain gives you impressive views of the city, the bay and the beaches below.

Football is practically a religion in Brazil. Any football fan should visit Maracana, which is the biggest stadium in the country and the site of the opening ceremony for the 2016 Olympics hosted by Rio.

Carnival in Rio is a fabulous riot of colour and costumes set to music and dancing. During Carnival, there is a published schedule outlining the Blocos (block parties held by different neighbourhoods). Join as

133

many Blocos as your party feet will stand. Friendly and happy, Cariocas are dancing to the music and more than happy to engage with tourists despite any language barrier. A separate children's Bloco is geared towards family-friendly fun. Don't worry about costumes – anything goes. There are street stalls selling cheap accessories to get into the spirit.

How about challenges?

You need to buy tickets to the Sambadrome Parades well in advance. There are four days of parades and the best samba schools are invited back to parade together on a fifth day. The sheer spectacle of these samba school dancers, costumes and floats is mind-blowing. It is readily apparent to anyone how much preparation and planning goes into creating such an extravagant display. The crowds happily show their appreciation! The enthusiasm Cariocas display will have you on your feet dancing.

The Sambadrome Parades start in the evening and go into the wee hours of the morning. Be sure to take a nap so that you aren't too exhausted to enjoy the parades! You will need to wait until about midnight to leave because most taxi drivers will take the nights off to party themselves. Regular shuttle buses run after midnight from the Sambadrome to the main tourist areas when you find your energy flagging.

Although we felt safe amidst the sea of humanity crowding around us during Carnival, we did take some sensible precautions. Don't draw attention to yourself by flashing the cash or wearing expensive jewellery. Have small change readily handy for buying drinks and souvenirs. Keep a secure grip on your camera too.

Who's it for?

Carnival is best for children are aged 10+ who will not be fearful of crowds and noise. Kids who love a party will be thrilled.

What are the kid-friendly experiences to seek out?

The best kid-friendly experiences include getting to see the Christ

the Redeemer statue up close and personal, taking a cable car to Sugarloaf Mountain for panoramic views of the city, playing on the famous beaches and visiting Maracanã Stadium. During Carnival, do check out the fun at the Children's Bloco party and the Carnival Parade at the Sambadrome.

Clockwise from top left: On Ipanema Beach; Rio viewed from Christ the Redeemer; Corcovado Mountain; getting into Carnival spirit.

SARAH STOCKING, LONELY PLANET WRITER

Skiing with kids in Colorado

What's it like to travel here as a family?

Skiing with your kids no matter the location can be a wonderful experience, but in the super-high peaks of Colorado, racing downhill as a family is like flying together as a flock of birds, the blue sky stretched out all around you and the soft white snow beneath your skis.

Tell us your favourite parts of the trip.

The many peaks in Colorado that range in height from 11 to 14,000 feet (3300 to 4200 metres) mean that by the time you've journeyed to the top of most of the ski areas, the views are breathtaking. Snow-covered mountain ranges stretch one after the other as far as the eye can see, and the small towns at the base are tailor-made for winter-wonderland accolades.

Learning anything new as a family is bonding. It doesn't matter if the parent already knows how to ski and the kids are working on learning, or if you're all starting at ground zero together, having this thing to talk about, get better at and enjoy together is like yarn knitting a family together. When we ski as a family, it is multi-generational and includes so much extended family that finding a partner for the chairlift is never an issue.

In Colorado, even on the coldest days, the sun comes out to warm you in a way it can only do when you're that close to it. White snow sparkles and glistens like it's been sprinkled with fairy dust and just beckons tiny racers to push their abilities. If the weather feels too cold or windy, there is always a cup of hot cocoa in the lodge, a roaring fire to play games in front of or a hot tub to splash around in.

How about challenges?

There is no doubt that skiing is hard. The conditions are challenging to prepare for, and sometimes learning something new can be extremely frustrating. My advice to you is to plan and pack well. Everyone should do a ski lesson. Having a professional teach the tips and tricks, even for half a day, takes the pressure off of family members to be the experts, freeing you up to be more patient with each other and more encouraging of progress.

Take your time. You don't have to bomb black diamonds in a day. Remember that the point is to have fun together. If you feel your

Clockwise from top left: Heading down Ajax Mountain in Aspen; skiing at Steamboat Springs; taking the lift up the mountain.

© GLADASSFANNY / GETTY IMAGES

frustration bubble up, stop and breathe in the clear, cold air. Look out at the view and take a moment to feel the cold on your cheeks. Or take a break. I like to stretch out in the snow on a sunny day and marvel at how blue the sky is.

But no one is going to learn anything if they are cold. Having the right gear is the most important factor in skiing. Start at your base layer. Find a good set of long underwear that is moisture wicking and warm, and get a set for the whole family. Next, you'll want a layer of fleece, both jacket and pants. The outer layer should be insulated snow pants and jacket that are made to keep wet snow away from your body. I also suggest neck protection,

waterproof gloves or mittens and a good pair of thin, but warm socks. Merino wool is great for socks. You'll wear a helmet, and if you don't have your own equipment, these are rentable, but you should bring a hat for after the slopes and try to find a balaclava that fits over your head, but under your helmet.

Who's it for?

Skiing is for families who love to adventure together. Outdoorsy types who don't mind rolling with whatever mother nature throws at them. I recommend everyone who wants to ski be in fairly good shape and enjoy learning to use their bodies in different ways. Even someone who may not want to hit the slopes every day can

also have a great time at the ski lodge. Relaxing with a good book by the fire while everyone else skis is a special kind of treat in the mountains.

What are the kid-friendly experiences to seek out?

Play games together on the hill. We like a version of leap frog where we ski one after the other down the slope. We also play who can spray snow the best. When you stop quickly and turn your skis it creates a rooster tail of snow.

Playing in the snow is so fun too. Take a day to go sledding or ice-skating. Or just build snow forts one day, rushing in for hot chocolate to warm up.

FAMILY TRAVEL HANDBOOK

BRONWYN LEEKS, SMITHS HOLIDAY ROAD

Vietnam with a wheelchair

What's it like to travel here as a family?

Vietnam is a sensational family-friendly destination with a perfect mix of culture, city, beach, mountains and a deep interesting history. The people are warm, friendly and inviting and adore children. There are so many great experiences to immerse your kids in, including learning a new language, trying new foods and stepping outside your comfort zone. It is relatively easy to get to and most visitors can use the new easy-to-get Vietnam E-visa.

Tell us your favourite parts of the trip.

Vietnam offers adventure and great ways for families to connect. I love that it allows us to step outside our usual life and learn and embrace difference. We spent time on the overnight train from the capital city of HCMC to Danang, which was the perfect adventure to connect with locals, witness some great scenery and spend time together. We booked the tickets easily online before we travelled and secured a comfy four-berth cabin for the 16-hour train ride.

If you are a foodie family then street food tours or cooking classes are a great way to learn about Vietnamese cuisine. We walked the streets of Hoi An with our great guide Ha, who encouraged us all to try new foods like rose dumplings and sesame paste soup and the best *bánh mì* we had ever had! Exploring with a local guide helps create strong community connections, and not only do you learn about the history of the food, you also learn about the people, who perhaps have owned the shop for the last century.

Watching the kids jump off the side of a boat to snorkel in the waters of the Cham Islands was a highlight of exploring Danang. The boat staff sat with the kids, explaining all about the marine life here in Vietnam and what the kids may spot in the water.

Another highlight was exploring the Mekong River region, with floating markets, motorbike riding through the countryside and visiting Buddhist temples with locals.

Who's it for?

Vietnam is for everyone. There are so many different experiences to enjoy and such a variety of

landscapes that museum and history buffs will be just as at home in HCMC as an outdoor adventure enthusiast is in Hue. It is a place where you can sit and relax on a beach or be in the water snorkelling near Hoi An. You can be riding the rails chatting with locals on the extensive train network throughout the whole country or on the back of a motorbike heading for the hills in Sapa. We suggest a month is perfect to explore from South to North, yet if you are like most families and just have school holidays, we suggest you pick either North or South to fully immerse yourself in the region's local experiences. Both have an immense amount to offer.

What about challenges?

As a family we explore with a wheelchair user and Vietnam is often tricky with wheelchair access. Sidewalks are often in disrepair and covered in bikes of all kinds. Traffic is also a bit unpredictable. We have a can-do attitude and have always found the local people willing to help us out when loading the wheelchair on and off trains or buses. They share our same attitude that we will find a way for everyone to be included. We also have a fussy eater, but thankfully they were pleased to find familiar fruits at the market, plain rice at restaurants and familiar snacks at the little local shops. Most of all, expect the unexpected and stay positive!

What are the kid-friendly experiences to seek out?

Balance out the temple visits and museums with a trip to something more child friendly like a water park! Danang has a great hot springs water park around 45 minutes from the city. Kids who love being on the water and at the beach will find plenty to love in this country. But when travelling with kids we always bring some travel games for the long waits at airports, bus rides or train rides. Our go-to game is Uno. Encourage the kids to write a travel journal as well. It's a great way to recall their favourite memories, writing down new language words they've learned and saving tickets, too.

Clockwise from top left: Sunset in Hoi An; a cyclist in Hoi An; travelling the coast by train; bowls of local food await the adventurous eater.

KAREN AKPAN, THE MOM TROTTER

COURTESY OF NANA LUCKHAM

Moroccan magic

What's it like to travel here as a family?

Morocco is one of the most amazing countries that my family and I have travelled to. As American citizens, a visa isn't required to visit Morocco which is one of the reasons why we chose to travel there. Morocco has a lot of culture, from the narrow-walled medinas filled with local vendors, to the Sahara Desert. There is so much for families to enjoy. Our family spent a few days in Fez, as well as went camping in the Sahara Desert, which is an experience that we all hold dear to our hearts.

Tell us your favourite parts of the trip.

Morocco is filled with culture and a mixture of several ethnic and religious groups as well. Our families spent time in the city, where we experienced lots of Jewish, African, Mediterranean and Arab culture, and then in the Sahara Desert where we went camping we experienced Berber culture. We didn't visit any museums or do any kid-specific activities, however what we did was try as much as possible to immerse ourselves in the culture. We stayed in the heart of the Medina of Fez where all the locals set up shop. This allowed us to walk around, shop for spices, souvenirs and more. It was also the perfect place to try local Moroccan cuisine as well as street food. Staying where the locals stay allowed us to experience Morocco like Moroccans, which was not only beneficial for the kids but also beneficial for us as a family. One of the things we did was a walking

tour of Fez where we stopped by a local school. Our kids were invited in and the kids sang a few songs for them while they tried to join in and sing with the kids as well. This was such a great experience for the kids to see how children in Morocco learn.

Our family bonded the most on this trip to Morocco during our time in the Sahara Desert. It was a very long drive, about 10 hours that we spent in the car without electronics. We played games such as I Spy, sang songs, made jokes, read books and just enjoyed each other's company. When we got to the desert, we spent some time learning about Berber culture and the kids made some new friends. They all played together even though they couldn't understand each other. Play truly has no language. We rode camels

to our campground and enjoyed the beauty and quietness of the desert. It was truly magical.

What about challenges?
The main languages spoken in Morocco are Arabic and French, and because I speak French, I was lucky enough to be able to communicate with most people that we came across. It is important to note that lots of tourists visit Morocco, so many people also speak English as well. We stayed in a riad and the attendant spoke English. Our tour guide and driver also spoke English, so they were able to explain everything to us. I don't foresee people having any language barrier issues while in Morocco, especially in tourist destinations.

The food in Morocco was some of the best and most flavourful we've had. Our family enjoyed every meal we had together. Our kids are open to trying new things, so they had no issue eating Moroccan food. Lots of places also serve foods like French fries and pasta, so if you have a very picky eater you will be able to find foods that they can eat.

Any words of advice?
I highly suggest planning ahead and/or booking a guide as needed. We booked a private driver before we arrived who picked us up at the airport and took us around to everywhere we needed to go. I also suggest checking the weather prior to heading to Morocco so that you can pack and plan activities appropriately. Also, if you're only spending a few days in Morocco, having an itinerary is great so that you have your days planned. It's also okay if you want to wing it, however, there is so much to see and do that you may get overwhelmed. Make sure to bargain prices at the market, but also be reasonable and considerate.

Who's it for?
Morocco is for everyone and anyone. Morocco is a very family-friendly destination for kids of all ages. I recommend it for families

who want to raise global citizens by immersing their children in a different culture. There's something to do in Morocco for everyone; you can visit the beach, stay at a resort and relax, enjoy the outdoors by hiking and camping, ride camels or sightsee and learn about the history. Morocco has so much variety, despite a daunting reputation.

Clockwise from top left: Visiting a school in Fez; camel train in the Sahara; meeting new friends; touring Fez by donkey.

What are the kid-friendly experiences to seek out?

Take a guided tour of whatever city you visit; guides know how to explain the history to kids in a way that will keep them intrigued and engaged. Do go camping in the Sahara Desert, an experience your family will treasure forever.

COURTESY OF KAREN APKA

147

KIRSTIE PELLING,
THE FAMILY ADVENTURE PROJECT

From left: Rome's Colosseum; the Eurostar before departure.

© JUSTIN FOULKES / LONELY PLANET

Biking across Europe by rail

What's it like to travel here as a family?

Interrail travel with kids is as challenging and as varied as a European rail timetable. Add folding bikes into the mix and you have an exhilarating adventure. We travelled from London to Istanbul, heading home via Athens and Rome. From fast trains to slow trains to no trains; a grand tour by rail.

Tell us your favourite parts of the trip.

Train travel is all about relaxation. Well, mostly. I'll admit there were stress-inducing moments at stations where our carriage rushed past us like an arrow from a bow, leaving us to marshal kids, bikes and luggage through impatient crowds to our allocated seats. Boarding was particularly tricky

on night trains where passengers destined for the sixth bunk panicked to find their luggage space consumed by our pedals and saddles. But like any travel, you soon get into a rhythm of loading and unloading, and we often drifted off to sleep to a lullaby of train on track. In the growing dusk, industrial buildings morphed into softer hills, then the sky widened and we dreamed we were moving as fast as the stars – until Bulgarian and Turkish border guards took control of our passports and our sleep.

Bringing five folding bikes proved a masterstroke. Our wheels freed us up to explore towns and cities. In Bucharest our three kids joined Sunday gamers chasing Pokémon Go characters around Herăstrău Park. In Vienna they conducted an orchestra at

the Haus der Musik interactive sound museum. In Budapest we bathed in Széchenyi Thermals with clusters of stags and hens, branded with tribal tiara and T-shirt. In Rome we cycled the perimeter of the Colosseum, and enjoyed a traffic-free approach to St Peter's Square during a storm that produced poncho sellers as fast as it diminished crowds. In Istanbul we took in Grand Bazaar and even grander Blue Mosque, and dined like kings on rich kebabs. In Athens we hung back at sunset as a golden Acropolis emptied and quieted, and the following day biked bleached-white back streets to catch a ferry to Aegina. In Venice we ditched the wheels; bikes are about as welcome as cars in a city populated by water taxis.

FAMILY TRAVEL HANDBOOK

How about challenges?

Planning felt like a full-time job in the months before departure. Fast trains and sleeper carriages required advance reservations and many had already sold out, thanks in part to Interrail offering free trips for Europeans turning 18. The Man in Seat 61 blog was a lifesaver, and the guy in the DB Deutsche Bahn call centre became my new best friend as I scrabbled to secure seats and bunks. Plans came together and then fell down if lines were closed, stations were being refitted, trains were swapped with rail replacement buses, or we could only buy tickets in person. Rail and accommodation logistics for 18 different cities kept me on my toes as I pulled together a scarily tight three week schedule. I feared if we missed just one train, the whole plan might collapse.

There were also challenges and comic moments on the move. Like the sweltering night train from Istanbul to Bucharest where the air conditioning failed and a kindly guard invited me to leave my sweat-soaked pillow for coffee in his carriage from his pristine silver kettle. And none of us will ever forget the chaos at the Eurostar terminal where a security official insisted on sending all five bikes through the scanners in trays, where they consecutively toppled like dominos.

Any words of advice?

Start your planning early; ideally at least a year in advance. Budget in the knowledge that your Interrail ticket, if you're using one, doesn't cover all costs. You will need to pay further fees to reserve seats on some routes and couchettes on night trains.

Who's it for?

The beauty of interrailing is it suits all ages. We met families with toddlers and others travelling with teens. Our teens loved the fast pace of the trip, and the variety of cities left no time for boredom. Wi-fi and charge points are available on many trains, and there's plenty of chill-out time built in. And if fussy eaters don't like the food in one country... there's always another on the way!

What are the kid-friendly experiences to seek out?

Arriving in iconic European cities at dusk was atmospheric. Cologne Cathedral was an unexpected gift as we exited the station for a between-trains cappuccino. In Istanbul the shops of the prosaic lighting district lit our path as brightly as the Galata Tower.

By day, we loved the street art tour of Sofia and tracking down the dog in the ruins of Pompeii. Our memories of guzzling wood-fired pizza in moody Naples are as vivid as those of wandering the shadowy alleys of Venice with cartons of takeaway pasta. It won't be our last trip combining bikes and rails!

Clockwise from top left: Istabul's harbour; inside the Hagia Sophia; Cologne cathedral; the spas in Budapest.

JADE JOHNSTON, OUR OYSTER

Camping in Tasmania

What's it like to travel here as a family?

Tasmania packs a lot into its small geographical size; wild places complete with mountains, forests, and beaches, world-class art and culture, loads of history and one of the best food and wine scenes in Australia. Tasmania is a laid back and friendly destination, making it a stress-free holiday option for families. Kids will love the wide-open spaces to play in and the parents will appreciate the fine wining and dining.

Tell us your favourite parts of the trip.

Despite being small, there is a lot on offer in Tasmania. The island can be broken down into five main regions: Hobart, the Tasman Peninsula, the East Coast, Launceston and the Tamar Valley, and Cradle Mountain.

Hobart is the cultural heart of the island, and home to the state capital and the island's largest city. Those travelling with kids that will tolerate art galleries will want to ensure to schedule in a visit to MONA – one of the world's most interesting contemporary art galleries. We spent half a day visiting the museum with our four-year-old and he was enthralled the entire time. We recommend picking up the free audio guide if you are travelling with kids. Being able to play around with the audio guide and hear the commentary about the different art works really held our four-year-old's attention and allowed us to keep him engaged and happy for a longer period. If you are visiting over the weekend, make sure to check out the Salamanca markets held every

Saturday at the waterfront.

The Tasman Peninsula is an easy day trip from Hobart, but we recommend spending a night or two. Here you will find dramatic coastline, interesting geological formations and one of Australia's most important historical sites – Port Arthur. Port Arthur is one of Australia's most important convict sites and is a Unesco World Heritage site. The entrance tickets are valid for 48 hours, which makes sense as there is so much to explore. We only had a couple of hours, which was definitely not enough time. There are also quite a few short and accessible little interpretative walks around this region, most of which are child friendly, and some that are even pram friendly.

The East Coast of Tasmania is a road tripper's dream. Here you will

From left:
Wineglass Bay
and Freycinet
National Park; a
local wallaby.

find some of the most stunningly beautiful coastline that the state has to offer, with the jewel in the crown being Wineglass Bay in Freycinet National Park. One hike not to miss is the 1.5-hour return hike up to Wineglass Bay Lookout. The walk is relatively easy but has quite a bit of incline. Our four-year-old did most of it without complaints, although my husband did carry him on his shoulders for some of the steeper sections. There are wonderful beaches all along the East Coast, but our favourite was right up at the top, at the Bay of Fires. We spent several days exploring the various beaches and rock pools there.

The Launceston and Tamar Valley region is famous for its vineyards, but there is still plenty around here to keep the kids busy. We spent a day driving the Tamar Valley food and wine tour and one of our favourite spots was the Hillwood Berry Farm. Here you can pick strawberries, raspberries, red currants, and the little ones will delight in searching out the juiciest ones. Our four-year-old had so much fun picking (and eating) the strawberries. So much so that he even remained relatively happy and allowed us to visit some of the vineyards in the region. In Launceston don't miss Cataract Gorge, which has a great swimming hole, lots of accessible walking paths and a fun chairlift which was a huge hit with our little one. We took it across the gorge one way, and then walked back along the various walking paths.

Of course, no trip to Tasmania would be complete without an excursion to Cradle Mountain. This region is beautiful no matter what season, and we visited in the winter when there was even a little bit of snow on the ground, which was a huge hit. For many Australian kids, a visit to Tasmania in the winter might be the first time they ever see snow. Cradle Mountain is famous for some of its challenging and rewarding hiking, but there are also lots of family-friendly options for all fitness levels. Two of our favourites were the Enchanted Walk which was a 20 minutes return walk along an accessible boardwalk,

and the 2- to 3-hour circuit hike around Dove Lake. Little ones will enjoy being outdoors, and there are lots of great opportunities to spot wildlife. We even shared one of our walks with a round little wombat.

Who's it for?

Families who love art and nature, and parents who enjoy wine-tasting, will find Tasmania answers all. Tasmania really does have something for everyone, but it really has a lot to offer for families who love to get out into the great outdoors. Whether it's hiking, camping or simply discovering beautiful beaches, Tasmania is a paradise for lovers of nature.

What about challenges?

Tasmania is a relatively easy place for families to travel to. But like any location where natural places and the wilderness are some of the main attractions, there will be some places which are not easily accessible for prams and strollers. If you are keen to get out and explore as much of the great outdoors as possible, and still have little ones in a buggy, then bring along a reliable child carrier to strap them onto.

Any words of advice?

Tasmania is a popular travel destination, and if you are planning to travel during an Australian school holiday period, then book things like

accommodation and ground transport well in advance, particularly for regional areas where accommodation options can be limited. Things like the Maria Island ferry have limited spots and should be booked as early as possible.

Tasmania is also a great place for camping holidays. We stayed at a couple of different family-friendly camp grounds along the East Coast, and our son loved the freedom, the kid-friendly facilities and, of course, being able to make friends with the other families staying there as well. Even if you are not a fan of camping, many of these spots do offer cabins for rent, which will give you the best of both worlds.

JESSICA RICE JOHNSON, ELCIE EXPEDITIONS

Indonesia under sail

© SOFYAN EFENDI / SHUTTERSTOCK

What's it like to travel here as a family?

Indonesia is the stuff of fairy tales – active volcanoes, deadly dragons, mystical temples – and its more than 17,500 islands made exploring it by cruising sailboat pretty ideal. Numerous anchorages, national parks and coastal villages provided loads of opportunities for our two families, travelling together aboard our boat Elcie, to truly experience Indonesia's natural places – above and below the water.

Tell us your favourite parts of the trip.

Craggy volcanoes rose from the ocean floor and vibrant reefs emerged beneath our hulls as we approached the Lesser Sunda Islands – Flores, Komodo, Lombok and Bali. Making landfall by boat

gives the feeling of a gradual entrance and you become a part of the landscape. Not only that, your accommodations and food are sorted, as you've brought your home with you! Once ashore, inland trips are easily arranged through small operators or national park offices.

In Flores, a 4am minibus zoomed us past waking villages perched on precipitous ridges along the way to Kelimutu National Park. Climbing the last bit on foot and peering over the edge into the three strangely coloured crater lakes was dreamlike. On the return from Kelimutu, our driver stopped at a funky seaside restaurant that only served rice and noodle dishes – *nasi goreng* and *mie goreng* - cooked over gas burners in two giant pots.

We opted to 'hunt dragons' on

Rinca (pronounced Rin-ja) Island, as it seemed to attract fewer crowds than the more popular Komodo Island. The oversized monitor lizards skulking around did not disappoint. An overnight stop on Padar Island provided superb hiking and by nightfall we swung on our anchor amongst a fleet of friendly tour boats, one tied to our stern. On the island of Komodo, we stopped at Pink Beach and discovered a garden of soft corals to snorkel on just past the small boat dock. Later that day, we drifted over Manta Alley and paddled above five giant rays gracefully circling beneath us. The following morning found the crew high atop Gili Lawa Darat for a sunrise breakfast looking over a sparkling bay towards Komodo Island.

In Lombok, a morning trip to

From left: Exploring off ship and on.

the market revealed a feast of local fruits and vegetables and was where we found much of our provisions – warm tempeh wrapped in banana leaves, beans and greens, onions and eggs. Lucky for us, the fresh eggs were held to a light before being sold to prevent cracking a chick into the frying pan! A motorbike, barely visible beneath its cargo, was a convenience store on wheels off to deliver fresh produce up the mountainside.

Once in Bali, we anchored in Serangan Harbor with front row seats for the Sanur Kite Competition. Immense kites, wrangled by teams of young men, filled the sky from sunrise to sunset. Ascending and descending in unison, awards were given for proficiency. Our teenage daughters were impressed that this was how young people would spend a school holiday in Bali. An inland trip to Ubud found us balancing between rice paddies that reflected the surrounding landscape. Intricately carved temples, the Sacred Monkey Forest, a funeral procession and small offerings everywhere rounded out our Bali experience.

What about challenges?

A Bahasa Indonesia language app (there are several available) taught us simple greetings and phrases prior to our arrival in the country. Nothing could get a group of kids giggling more than counting Satu-Dua-Tiga (one-two-three) before performing some silly act for them. The Hypermarkets were generally slim on healthy and recognisable food unless you were looking for cooking oil, noodle packets or odd-looking snacks (what we called 'wacky snacks'), so the local markets provided more accessible food for us along with a great visual experience and a chance to practise the language.

Travelling under sail presented us with some typical cruising boat challenges. Several times, winds funnelling off of steep islands made for a wild ride into a harbour. We took to calling the country 'Windonesia'. Also, there was an extraordinary amount of small boat traffic to watch out

for. At night, an unlit boat would make itself known only when noisily motoring out of our direct path. However, these *Waterworld*-like craft were intriguing, and more than once we shared an anchorage with brightly painted local fishing and tour boats.

Who's it for?

On this journey from Flores to Bali, our five youngest crew ranged from age nine to 17. Indonesia is for the adventure-minded and this group was keen to do most anything that presented itself, including summiting the highest hills, diving with manta rays and stalking Komodo dragons. With few dangerous animals (save those toothy Komodos) and relatively safe crime-wise, this area of Indonesia was a fairly relaxing place to travel with teenage (and nearly teenage) kids.

Any words of advice?

Allow enough time to explore at a leisurely pace. There is always going to be something to derail the schedule, making it hard to stick to a firm timetable. Check for the wet vs dry seasons in the areas you are travelling. We arrived in northern Indonesia a bit too early and spent a week hunkered down on board during torrential rains. One must also be aware of geologic dangers such as recent volcanic activity at Mount Agung on Bali and earthquake activity.

What are the kid-friendly experiences to seek out?

A kayak, two paddleboards and snorkel gear provided plenty of watery entertainment. Ukulele strumming, preparing meals and snacks from local ingredients, face painting and card games filled out the time aboard *Elcie*. Equally unforgettable was stargazing into the darkest of night skies and dolphin spotting.

Ashore, the hum of villages and local markets, sunrise hikes, an underwater world, rounding a corner to surprise a dragon or troop of monkeys and every warung that served its own version of *mie goreng* and *nasi goreng* made our journey through Indonesia excellent.

NANA LUCKHAM, LONELY PLANET WRITER

Tulum with a toddler

What's it like to travel here as a family?

Squeezed between jungly scrub and the bright blue waters of the Caribbean Sea, this small town on the Yucatán Peninsula has grown from a secret backwater into one of Mexico's coolest spots. But amongst the fashion parties, DJs and yoga studios there's plenty of space for families too.

Tell us your favourite parts of the trip.

For a first holiday away with our toddler son, Tulum served up the laid-back trip we were looking for, though the town has certainly moved on from its hippy days when the town was a dirt road and some simple shacks. The short stretch of beachside road is packed with small hotels and restaurants and

the vibe is more Coachella than Woodstock – but the stretch of powder-white sand looked as good as we expected and came as welcome respite after a couple of days in built-up Cancun.

There are three main parts to Tulum: the town, the beach (where most people stay) and the pre-Colombian Mayan site, whose dreamy position on a cliff overlooking the ocean is straight out of a kids' adventure book. There's no getting away from the fact that accommodation on the beach is expensive, so the town is a great alternative for cash-strapped parents. We stayed in two different places – a petite thatched hut right on the sand with an eye-watering price tag and a huge self-catering apartment in town that cost considerably less but had a lot more kid-friendly amenities.

The town is 3km (under 2 mile) away from the beach and has less of a 'scene', with a clutch of simple bars, restaurants and taco stands, as well as quiet side roads filled with street art. Many hotels offer shuttles to the beach, but we hired bikes complete with child seat and wheeled our way down the off-road track from town to the beach every day. Our favourite memories are of long walks by the sea, with the incredible blue of the sky over our heads and our son running wild on the sands.

Yes, there are a few adults-only hotels by the beach and some places definitely had a romantic couples feel to them, but most places were happy to accommodate us. We took our son everywhere – the restaurants are welcoming, chilled out and open air – so he could play at

161

our feet or swing in a hammock; and in the evenings he'd fall asleep on our laps or in his buggy while we drank a mezcal or two and attempted to relive our lost youth.

What about challenges?

Tulum is a pretty easy destination for a family. English is spoken everywhere, supermarkets stock plenty of international as well as local goodies and many restaurants can provide high chairs for your little ones. That being said, there were a few niggles that we came across.

Tulum's beach is off-grid, for example, so hotels, bars and restaurants use generators to keep the electricity going – leading to low water pressure, dim lights, patchy wi-fi and a lack of air-conditioning. If any of these are important to you, then you're best off staying in town.

With Tulum's increased popularity has also come huge amounts of traffic, which can move at a snail's pace along the main beach road in high season. While we hired a car for excursions further away, we found it much easier to get around the town and down to the beach by bike – just watch out for the cars once you're off the path and on the main beach road.

We also found that the ocean, while gorgeous to look at, wasn't that calm, so not great

for inexperienced swimmers. Not so much of a problem with a toddler, but I'd keep an eye on older children in the water. Also take care in the cenotes – natural swimming holes – found outside the town. These are deep, often have steep access and there are no sides to hang on to so armbands or a life jacket are a must for kids, even if they already know how to swim.

Any words of advice?

Tulum is popular, so you need to get your accommodation sewn up early. And choose your hotel wisely – the increasing number of party places means noise can be an issue. Opt for town if you want more peaceful nights.

Who's it for?

Families with kids of all ages can enjoy Tulum but it helps if you love being outdoors. Babies and toddlers can happily spend all day playing in the sand and splashing in the shallows; older kids will love the cenotes, scrambling over Mayan ruins, swimming with turtles at nearby Akumal and seeing monkeys and crocs at the Sian Ka'an biosphere reserve. Teenagers will probably want to ditch their parents to check out some of the nightlife.

What are the kid-friendly experiences to seek out?

The best thing to do in Tulum? Just hang out. We could easily have spent the whole time biking around the town and the beach, people watching, trying all the excellent food and just enjoying life on the sands. Outside of town, a visit to a cenote is a magical experience for kids, and they'll be equally delighted clambering over the local Mayan ruins, both in Tulum, where there's the added bonus of dramatic ocean views, and at Coba, around an hour away, where you can whizz around the crumbling pyramids in a pedicab.

Clockwise from top left: Chichen Itza's pyramid; incredibly blue waters; Sian Ka'an turtle viewing.

163

BRYANNA ROYAL, CRAZY FAMILY ADVENTURE

RVing the USA

What's it like to travel in an RV as a family?

There is nothing like packing your family into your 'home on wheels' to head out on the open road. You can't beat the excitement of a road trip, and what better way to do it than in an RV where you have the luxury of a fridge and beds on board. Spend your nights surrounded by nature, then in the morning open your door for an amazing sunrise and breakfast with gorgeous views. Being in nature is an awesome way to reconnect with your family.

Tell us your favourite parts of the trip.

The western US makes an unforgettable RV road trip. There is so much open space and so many amazing national parks that you can visit. Each region here has its own amazing highlights.

Head to Utah for unbelievable scenery filled with red rocks and arches. There are times you will feel like you are on a different planet with the strange, yet beautiful landscape that covers the state. Visit five National Parks and one of our favourite State Parks, Goblin Valley, on the ultimate Utah Road Trip.

For epic mountain views, turquoise-blue glacier water, geysers shooting to the sky and wild animals, head into Yellowstone, Grand Tetons and Glacier National Parks. If you are coming from the east, make a stop at Mount Rushmore and the Badlands on the way in.

Be blown away by the huge waterfalls and gigantic trees of California and the beautiful greenery and rugged coast of Oregon. Head to Yosemite, the Redwoods, Crater Lake and the Oregon coast for an amazing road trip. You really can't go wrong with a West Coast RV trip. Plus national parks have the awesome Junior Ranger programs where kids can complete a workbook to earn Junior Ranger badges.

You'll find unlimited hiking for all age and skill levels and plenty of rocks for kids to scramble up. You can also find a variety of tours for rafting, horseback riding, rock climbing and off-roading.

Feeling really adventurous? Look into boondocking where you stay for free on public land with no hookups!

Who's it for?

RV travel is for families with young kids, older kids and everyone in between who want to experience

the beautiful outdoors without having to stay in a tent. You don't have to be super adventurous or willing to rough it. There are some pretty luxurious RVs out there. Or you can choose to go with a more rustic rig. The choice is yours.

Part of the joy of an RV trip is having downtime to just enjoy nature, so don't cram your days with constant activities. Stock up on marshmallows and fun meals to cook over the campfire, and make the trip not just about the destination but also about the experience of camping itself! Have a loose schedule that allows you to stay up late around the campfire eating s'mores and stargazing and then sleep in the next morning. An RV road trip is a trip your whole family will never forget.

What about challenges?

Selecting an RV can sometimes be the biggest hurdle of all. Before picking your RV, plan your route and then research campgrounds and check size restrictions at the places you want to stay. National Parks and State Parks can have length restrictions for RVs. Doing your route and campground research up front will help you decide what size RV to rent. If you are new to RVing try to go with a smaller rig – under 30 feet for easier driving and mobility.

If you have never driven an RV before or don't know how to hook one up at a campsite, there can be a learning curve. Never fear, the RVing community is super friendly and helpful and there are always people around the campgrounds to answer questions. Plus when you rent an RV, companies give you a rundown on how everything works. And there is always YouTube, where lots of great informational videos can be found on RVing.

One of the great things about RVing is when it is time to move on to the next location, you have everything with you. No need to pack and unpack a suitcase; everything is right there with you ready to hit the road. Have allergy

or diet restrictions? No problem. You can stock your RV fridge before you go and cook your meals in your RV kitchen with a microwave, stovetop and oven. Once you have got into the swing of setup and takedown you will wonder why you didn't do this sooner!

Any words of advice?

Stay at a campground in the national park you are visiting. It gives a whole different experience to being in a national park if you can start your day right in the middle of the park surrounded by the gorgeous views. Wake up, eat breakfast and head out to explore!

Clockwise from top left: From Oregon to Yellowstone and Mt Washburn; beware the bears!

Published in January 2020 by Lonely Planet Global Limited
CRN 554153
www.lonelyplanet.com
ISBN 978 1 7886 8915 1
© Lonely Planet 2020
Printed in China
10 9 8 7 6 5 4 3 2 1

Publishing Director Piers Pickard
Associate Publisher Robin Barton
Commissioning Editor Nora Rawn
Author Imogen Hall
Art Director Daniel Di Paolo
Print Production Nigel Longuet
Cover illustration © Niki Fisher

STAY IN TOUCH lonelyplanet.com/contact

AUSTRALIA The Malt Store, Level 3, 551 Swanston St,
Carlton, Victoria 3053 T: 03 8379 8000

IRELAND Digital Depot, Roe Lane (off Thomas St),
Digital Hub, Dublin 8, D08 TCV4

USA 124 Linden St, Oakland, CA 94607
T: 510 250 6400

UNITED KINGDOM 240 Blackfriars Rd, London SE1 8NW
T: 020 3771 5100

Although the authors and Lonely Planet have taken all reasonable care in preparing this book, we make
no warranty about the accuracy or completeness of its content and, to the maximum extent permitted,
disclaim all liability from its use.

Paper in this book is certified against the Forest Stewardship Council™
standards. FSC™ promotes environmentally responsible, socially beneficial
and economically viable management of the world's forests.